9.95

TOUT de SUITE à la MICROWAVE II

by
JEAN K DURKEE

D1469223

A gourmet's cookbook
of
Mexican, Italian & French
recipes

1st printing   November, 1980   60,000 copies
2nd printing   June, 1981   80,000 copies

Library of Congress Catalog Card Number 80-53827
ISBN 0-9605362-1-3

Copyright © 1980 by Jean K. Durkee
Tout de Suite à la Microwave II
P. O. Box 30121
Lafayette
Louisiana
70503

To Bob and our sons Robert, Mark and Todd
who watched with pride and amazement
as *Tout de Suite I* circulated
nation-wide.
To my parents, parents-in-law and brother
and especially my loyal staff members
for "behind the scene" support.

With their encouragement
Tout de Suite II
was created.

ACKNOWLEDGEMENTS

Recipes developed and tested by
Jean K. Durkee and Jolene M. Levermann

Illustrations
Randy Herpin

Photography
Cover: John C. Guillet
Back Cover: Paul Skipworth
Candid: Sheryn Jones
John C. Guillet

Editorial Consultants
Sheryn Jones
Orpha Valentine

Typists
Alyce Tatum and Rose Must

Microdry flowers by
Lucy S. Kellner

Spanish translation
Carolyn Greco

Italian translation
Jerry Vroegh

French translation
Dave Domingue

Published by
Tout de Suite à la Microwave, Inc.
P. O. Box 30121
Lafayette, Louisiana 70503

Printed in U.S.A.
S.C. Toof & Co.
670 S. Cooper St.
Memphis, TN 38104

INTRODUCTION

Buenas días, *Buon giorno*, *Bonjour* to 200,000 friends across the 50 states and many foreign countries microwaving with *Tout de Suite à la Microwave I & II*.

Recipes from around the world are the basis of American cooking. *Tout de Suite à la Microwave II*, using a new method of cooking, captures all the traditional flavors of Mexican ⬛, Italian 🐓 , and French ⚜ food. These symbols are used for easy recognition on pages with the recipe title translation.

Jolene M. Levermann, who has helped me give hundreds of cooking schools across the United States, assisted me in testing all of the 210 recipes in the Tout de Suite kitchen using 675–700 watt counter top microwave ovens. The Consumer Appliance Section of the International Microwave Power Institute is working on standardization of variable power level settings. The settings proposed are: 100% (High), approximately 70% (Medium-High), 50% (Medium), approximately 30% (Low) and approximately 10% (Warm). *Tout de Suite II* recipes use these settings.

We converted more than 95% of the recipes to microwave cooking from favorite recipes of friends and family listed in the back of the book. Also, several friends who are home economists, Ann Steiner, CiCi Williamson, Mary Beth Cyvas, Pat Freeman, Lorraine Keowen and Billie Hebert shared recipes they converted to the microwave. Many friends, along with our husbands, Bob and Charley, helped taste the array of recipes prepared each evening.

Many of the south of the border recipes were collected by Jolene when she lived in Maracaibo, Venezuela and in south Texas. Others were inspired by my visits to Acapulco, Cozumel, Mazatlán and Monterrey, Mexico. An interest in Italian cooking was broadened by Julie Dannenbaum's cooking school at The Greenbrier and Marco de Grazia of Florence, Italy. My repertoire of French cooking from all areas of France was heightened by Mrs. Connett's Chateau Country Cooking School in the quaint and delightful village of Chinon, France and also, Le Cordon Bleu and LaVarenne in Paris.

Cookbooks should not be just for cooking, but for increasing our knowledge and understanding of people and places. I hope, through my enthusiasm for microwave cooking, using recipes from Mexico, Italy and France, you will be inspired to experiment with recipes from other countries, using *Tout de Suite I & II* as a guide.

Jean Kellner Durkee

Table of Contents

UTENSILS

Many new microwave utensils are available now for cooking and serving. The following list is a supplement to the utensil chart in *Tout de Suite à la Microwave I*.

UTENSIL OR CONTAINER	SIZE	A FEW OF THE RECIPES USING THESE UTENSILS
Glass measuring cups with handle	1 cup 2 cup 4 cup 8 cup	Measuring cups were repeated because all 4 sizes are excellent for microwave cooking. 1 & 2 cup for sauce and sautéing. 2 cup for pumpkin bread, 4 cup for roux, 8 cup for divinity.
Round glass plate for cooking and serving	12"	Vegetable medley, oysters Reagan, sausage stuffed mushrooms, turkey, also doubles as a cake plate.
Glass ring shape dish for cooking and serving	1 quart 1½ quart	Mexican bread pudding, prosciutto broccoli mousse, salad molds, cakes.
Glass mixing bowls for cooking and serving	1 quart 3 quart 4 quart	Sauces, Mexican dip, hot crab appetizer, Creole bread dressing, omelet, coffee cake, melting chocolate, frostings, pralines, creamy peach ice cream.
Round glass casserole for cooking and serving	2 quart 3 quart	Steamed rice, all casseroles, baking bread, oyster and shrimp jambalaya.
Glass baking dish for cooking and serving	7" × 11"	Enchiladas, lasagna, Cajun shrimp bake, turkey, roast, peanut butter sighs.
Corning casseroles for cooking and serving	3 quart 4 quart 5 quart	This was repeated because all 3 sizes are excellent. Seafood gumbo II, turkey gumbo, green pepper jelly, pinto and red beans.
Porcelain Bundt dish Porcelain gratin dish	12 cup 6 ounce	Bundt cakes Creamed chicken, asparagus, escargot Monaco, all individual servings.
Microwave safe plastic cake or casserole pie plate	9" 9"	"Micro Magic" combination cake, casserole and pie plate that doubles as a lid. Unit also includes a rack and 6 muffin cups.
Plastic colander		Cook and drain ground meat in one step.
Clay pot for cooking and serving	2 quart 3 quart	Water soaked for roast duck, chicken and quail.
Portable food rotator	wind up handle	Even cooking, eliminates hand turning of food.

MICRO MEMOS

The following micro memos are helpful hints for microwave cooking. Twenty other micro memos, which pertain to the recipe, are included throughout the book.

TESTING DISH: To test a dish for safe microwave cooking, place the empty dish to be tested in the microwave oven. Place a 2-cup glass measuring cup filled with one cup of water in or beside the dish. Microwave on **HIGH (100%) 2 MINUTES.** If dish remains cool it is considered microwave safe.

BROWNING DISH: Browning dishes for searing and browning food come in a variety of sizes. The most versatile is a 9-inch square with a lid. The coating imbedded on the bottom of the dish absorbs microwave energy when the empty browning dish is heated, which causes the dish to reach temperatures of 500 to 600°F. Because of the high heat from the dish, use a lid to cover but never wax paper or paper towels which could catch fire. Add butter, margarine or oil instead of non-stick spray after dish has been preheated ⅔ of the time. Dish cleans quickly with baking soda.

FOIL USAGE: Check your owner's manual on foil usage. Narrow strips of foil shield areas from overcooking, see page 89 for example. The mass of food must be greater than the amount of foil used.

COVERS: 1) Thin **plastic wrap** that stretches not shrinks can be used for foods that need to be covered tightly and steamed. Plastic wrap can be vented at one corner in recipes which minimize steaming. 2) **Wax paper** tented or loosely covered helps distribute heat for more even cooking and prevents spattering. 3) **Paper towel** absorbs excess moisture and allows steam to escape. Wrap bread to be warmed or thawed in a paper towel. 4) **Container lid** with a loose fit lets some steam escape. For a tighter fit place a sheet of wax paper between lid and dish.

COOKING BAGS: Heavy duty Brown-In-Bags cook meat and poultry evenly. Thin plastic bags are good for foods with short cooking times, such as potatoes. Puncture potato with a fork, place in plastic bag, hand-twist end of bag and place on a microsafe plate. Microwave on **HIGH (100%) 4 MINUTES** per 1 medium potato.

DEFROSTING: If meat is packed on a styrofoam tray, remove as soon as possible when defrosting meat. The tray acts as an ice chest by insulating bottom of item being defrosted.

CLEANING OVEN: To clean inside of microwave oven, place 1 cup of water with a squeeze of lemon juice or a teaspoon of vanilla or almond extract in microwave on **HIGH (100%) 2 MINUTES.** Use a dry cloth to wipe inside of oven clean. Gives kitchen a nice aroma, too!

MICRO DRY FLOWERS

The microwave oven is a time saver in preparing a wide variety of foods. Along with its speed and convenience, Lucy S. Kellner has found it to be great for other things, such as drying flowers. Here is a list of items and techniques you will need in drying your own flowers.

WHEN TO PICK FLOWERS Mid-morning after dew has dried or until 2 o-clock in afternoon is the best time to pick flowers for micro drying. Pick flowers just before they reach their peak of bloom and micro dry as soon as possible. If flower is picked as a bud, place stem in water overnight.

CHOOSING FLOWERS TO DRY Flowers with short sturdy petals that are bright in color are easy to dry. Among these are roses, zinnias, pansies, chrysanthemums, corn flower, daffodils and marigolds.

SUPPLIES AND MATERIALS NEEDED Flowers, fresh from garden or florist fresh. . . Silica Gel, available at craft or hobby shops (use 1 pound per 8–10 flowers) . . . unwaxed paper cups, paper shoe box, glass cups or bowls . . . green 20 gauge florist wire and green floral tape . . . scissors . . . wooden picks . . . soft paint brush . . . clear protective spray . . . glass cup filled with water to be placed in corner of microwave oven.

SIX EASY STEPS After selecting flowers to be dried and the container to be used, follow these 6 easy instructions for drying flowers.
1. Clip stem, leaving about ½ to 1 inch attached to flower. Insert a small wooden pick through stem. This will be removed after drying so florist wire may be attached.
2. Place flower stem-down into unwaxed paper cup or bowl which has been partially filled with silica gel to hold flower upright. A shoe box lid can be used as a tray for 10 small paper cups.
3. Spoon silica gel evenly between petals until every space has been filled. Shake cup gently to settle gel. Cover flowers completely with silica gel so that no petals are exposed.
4. Place a 1-cup glass measuring cup filled with water in the back corner of microwave. Follow the Micro Dry Chart for microwave cooking time on HIGH (100%) power. Use chart as a guide for flowers you would like to dry that are not listed. Try experimenting with flowers from your own garden and wildflowers from your area and continue the chart.
5. After micro drying flowers let stand until cup and gel are cool, about 20 to 30 minutes. Flowers may be left in gel overnight. Silica gel can be reused many times. Cool completely before using again. Remove small flowers from gel at 5 minutes.
6. After flowers have cooled, carefully remove from silica gel and place on a cake rack, using a soft brush to remove dust from flowers. Make stems with florists wire cut in various lengths. Remove wooden picks and hook wire through hole made with pick. Secure wire to stem by wrapping with green floral tape.

MICRO DRY FLOWER CHART
by
Lucy S. Kellner

FLOWERS		MICRO DRY ON HIGH (100%)	UTENSILS
3 stems	Baby Breath	3 minutes	Shoe box with 2″ silica gel
1 branch	Bougainvillaea	3 minutes	Shoe box with 2″ silica gel
3	Carnations	2½ minutes	3 large paper cups**
7 small	Chrysanthemums	80 seconds	7 small paper cups
1 large	Chrysanthemum	3 minutes	Large bowl . . . let stand overnight
8 small	Blue Corn Flower	80 seconds	8 small paper cups
1	Daffodil	2 minutes	Large paper cup
8 small	Marigolds	80 seconds	8 small paper cups
7–8	Pansies	45 seconds . . . repeat 90 seconds	7–8 small paper cups
1 large	Rose bud	80 seconds	Large paper cup
8–10	Mercedes Rose	80 seconds	8–10 small paper cups
1 small	Orchid	1 minute	1 small paper cup
8–10	Sweetheart roses	80 seconds	8–10 small paper cups
10–20	Rose petals	90 seconds	Shoe box
1 bunch	Purple Statice	90 seconds	Shoe box
1 bunch	Seafoam Statice	90 seconds	Shoe box
1	Sun Flower	1 minute 45 seconds	Large bowl or dish. Let stand 1½ days covered in plastic
6 stalks	Wheat	80 seconds	Shoe box
1 bunch	Yarrow	90 seconds	Shoe box
7 small	Zinnias	80 seconds	7 small paper cups
1 large	Zinnia	90 seconds	Large paper cup or glass jar
branch of 3 clean	Fall Leaves	1½ min. turn over . . . repeat 1½ min.	Layer with paper towels not silica gel in shoe box or dish
10–15 stalks	Monkey Grass	1½ min. turn over . . . repeat 1½ min.	Layer with paper towels not silica gel. May turn brown in 6 months
4–6	*Cut-Leaved Daisy	80 seconds	4–6 paper cups
4–6	*Fire-Wheel	80 seconds	4–6 paper cups
4–6	*Green Lily	80 seconds	Shoe box
4–6	*Heather	90 seconds	4–6 paper cups
4–6	*Scarlet Paintbrush	90 seconds	4–6 paper cups

*Texas wildflowers dried by Sheryn Jones   **Use unwaxed paper cups only

Hors d' oeuvre

Hors d'oeuvre:

*In any language, hors d'oeuvre, antojitos or antipastos . . .
appetizers are meant only to tease not satisfy.*

ARTICHOKE NIBBLES
délices d'artichauts

Cooking Time: 11 minutes
Utensils: 2-cup glass measuring cup
        7 x 11-inch glass baking dish
Servings: 60–70 squares

**2 (6-oz.) jars marinated
   artichoke hearts
1/2 cup onions, chopped
2 cloves garlic, minced**

1. Drain liquid from 1 jar of arti-chokes into a 2-cup measure. Add onions and garlic. Sauté on **HIGH (100%) 2 to 3 MINUTES** until on-ions are soft. Chop artichokes, re-serving liquid from second jar for a salad.

**4 eggs
1/4 cup seasoned bread
   crumbs
1/4 teaspoon salt
1/8 teaspoon red pepper
1/8 teaspoon oregano
1/8 teaspoon Tabasco
2 Tablespoons parsley,
   minced
1/2 pound Cheddar cheese,
   grated**

2. Beat eggs in a mixing bowl. Add crumbs, salt, pepper, oregano, Ta-basco and parsley. Stir in cheese, chopped artichokes and sautéed onions. Pour into a greased 7 x 11-inch baking dish. Microwave on **HIGH (100%) 7–8 MINUTES**. Rotate dish 2 times. Let stand 5 minutes before slicing into 1-inch squares. Serve hot or cold.

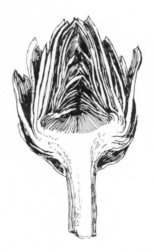

CHEDDAR CHEESE SQUARES

quadrilles de cheddar

Cooking Time: 4 minutes 30 seconds
Utensils: Cover a 12-inch round piece of cardboard with wax
paper for baking sheet
Trivet
Servings: 30–36 pieces

1/3 cup margarine, cold
3/4 cup Cheddar cheese,
grated, cold
3/4 cup all-purpose flour
1/4 teaspoon salt
1/4 teaspoon Tabasco

1. Using a food processor cream margarine and cheese with steel blade. Add flour, salt and Tabasco. Process on/off until mixture is crumbly then process just until mixture forms a ball on top of blade. Chill dough 5 minutes.

2. Sprinkle flour on prepared 12-inch round baking sheet. Press dough onto center of sheet. Cover with another sheet of wax paper and roll out dough to fit baking sheet. Elevate* baking sheet on a trivet rack or turntable. Microwave uncovered on **HIGH (100%) 4 MINUTES 30 SECONDS**. Rotate baking sheet once or twice.

3. While still warm and soft, cut in desired shape: squares, sticks or rectangles. Let cool on baking sheet 5 minutes. Transfer to serving plate.

MICRO MEMO:

*Elevating the baking sheet helps pastry bake evenly by putting it into a pattern or area of more microwave energy.

CHEESE CHILI DIP
chile con queso para sopear

Cooking Time: 14 minutes 30 seconds
Utensils: Plastic colander
          2-quart glass dish
Servings: Makes 1 quart

1 pound lean ground beef
1 cup onions, chopped

1. Place meat and onions in a plastic colander over a 2-quart dish. Cover with wax paper. Microwave on **HIGH (100%) 5–6 MINUTES**, stirring at 2 minutes to break up lumps. Discard fat and return meat to dish.

2 Tablespoons flour
3 Tablespoons chili powder
2 jalapeño peppers, seeded
    and chopped
1 teaspoon garlic salt
1/4 teaspoon comino (cumin)
1/4 teaspoon oregano
1 cup water
3 cups mild Cheddar cheese,
    grated

2. Stir flour, chili powder, jalapeño peppers, garlic salt, comino (cumin), oregano and water into meat. Microwave on **HIGH (100%) 8 MINUTES 30 SECONDS**. Stir cheese into hot mixture, let sit 10 minutes. Serve with tortilla chips.

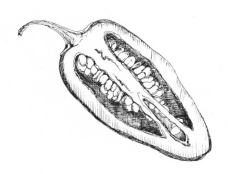

CHILAQUILES

Tortillas in chili sauce

Cooking Time: 10 minutes
Utensil: 7 x 11-inch glass baking dish
Servings: 8

1 medium onion, sliced in rings
1 Tablespoon vegetable oil
1 (10-oz.) can Ro-tel tomatoes and green chilies, chopped with liquid
1 (14½-oz.) can whole tomatoes, drained and chopped
1½ teaspoons salt
12 corn tortillas, cut into 1/2-inch wide strips

4 ounces Monterey Jack cheese, sliced in 2-inch strips
4 jalapeño peppers, quartered in strips and seeded

1. Place onion and oil in a 7 x 11-inch baking dish covered with plastic wrap. Microwave on **HIGH (100%) 5 MINUTES** until tender. Add tomatoes and salt. Place tortilla strips in tomato mixture tossing to mix. Cover with plastic wrap. Microwave on **HIGH (100%) 3 MINUTES**, stirring once.

2. Add cheese and jalapeño pepper slices on top of Chilaquiles. Cover with plastic wrap and microwave on **HIGH (100%) 2 MINUTES**. Cut in squares to serve.

CRAB DIP

crème de crabe

Cooking Time: 11 minutes
Utensils: 3-quart glass casserole
Servings: Makes 6 cups

1/2 cup margarine
1 cup onions, finely chopped
1 stalk celery, finely chopped
1 Tablespoon parsley

1. Micromelt margarine in a 3-quart casserole on **HIGH (100%) 1 MINUTE**. Add onions, celery and parsley. Microwave on **HIGH (100%) 5 MINUTES**.

1/2 pound Velvetta cheese,
cut in small pieces
1/2 cup evaporated milk
1/3 cup cream of mushroom
soup, undiluted
1/4 teaspoon garlic powder
1/8 teaspoon thyme
1/4 teaspoon red pepper
1 pound white crabmeat,
thawed and checked for
shells

2. Stir in cheese, milk, mushroom soup, garlic powder, thyme and red pepper. Fold in crabmeat gently. Microwave on **HIGH (100%) 5 MINUTES**, stirring once.

1/2 cup seasoned bread
crumbs

3. Stir in enough bread crumbs for desired thickness.

ESCARGOT MONACO

Cooking Time: 4 minutes
Utensils: 6 individual ceramic casseroles *or*
 2 glass pie plates
Servings: 6 (4 each)

1/2 cup margarine, softened
4 cloves garlic, minced
1 teaspoon Creole seasoning

1. Using the back of a spoon combine margarine, garlic and Creole seasoning. Spread half the mixture on the bottom of 6 individual casseroles *or* 2 pie plates.

24 large fresh mushroom
 crowns
2 (4¾-oz.) cans large snails
 (12 each)
4 Tablespoons white wine
1/2 cup Parmesan cheese,
 grated
4 Tablespoons parsley,
 snipped

2. Spread mushroom crowns with remaining garlic margarine and place 4 mushrooms in each individual casserole *or* 12 in each pie plate. Drain and rinse snails. Fill each mushroom with 1 snail. Sprinkle with wine, Parmesan cheese and parsley. Cover with plastic wrap and refrigerate until ready to cook and serve. Keep dishes covered when cooking. **For 6 individual casseroles**: Microwave 3 casseroles at a time on **HIGH (100%) 2 MINUTES**. **OR For 2 pie plates**: Microwave 1 plate at a time on **HIGH (100%) 2 MINUTES**. Serve with French bread.

GREEN PEPPER JELLY

jalea chile verde

Spread over cream cheese.

Cooking Time: 10–12 minutes
Utensils: 5-quart ceramic casserole
          6 (8-oz.) glass jars
Servings: 6

1/4 cup hot green peppers, Anaheim or Jalapeño, seeded and finely chopped or ground
3/4 cup green bell pepper, seeded and finely chopped or ground
6½ cups sugar
1½ cups apple cider vinegar

1. Mix ground peppers and their juices with sugar and vinegar in a 5-quart casserole. Cover and bring to a boil on **HIGH (100%) 10–12 MINUTES**, stirring once. Let stand 5 minutes.

6 ounces Certo liquid fruit pectin
2 or 3 drops green food coloring

2. Add liquid fruit pectin and 2 or 3 drops of green food coloring. Stir well. Pour into hot sterilized jars, seal with lids and store in refrigerator.

This jelly is marvelous as an hors d'oeuvre spread over cream cheese and crisp crackers. It is an excellent condiment for lamb, fowl, beef, pork or wild game.

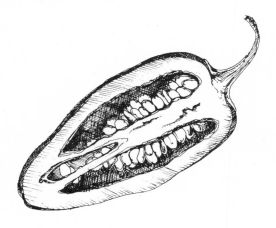

HOT CRAB ANTOJITO

antojito caliente de cangrejo
Pronounced ahn-toh-HEE-toh

A quick appetizer.

Cooking Time: 2 minutes 15 seconds
Utensils: Mixing bowl
          3 paper plates
Servings: Makes 45

**1 pound white crabmeat,
  flaked**
**3/4 cup Monterey Jack
  cheese with hot
  peppers, grated**
1/4 cup dairy sour cream
1/2 cup mayonnaise
**1 Tablespoon green onion,
  bulb minced**
**1 Tablespoon fresh lemon
  juice**
1 Tablespoon white wine
1/2 teaspoon salt
1/4 teaspoon cayenne pepper
1/4 teaspoon Tabasco
**Melba rounds, plain, garlic or
  onion**

1. Place crabmeat, after removing any shell pieces, in a 2-quart mixing bowl. To crabmeat add hot pepper cheese, sour cream, mayonnaise, onion, lemon juice, wine, salt, pepper and Tabasco. Toss lightly with 2 forks to mix. Spoon mixture on Melba rounds. Place 15 rounds on a paper plate (double plates if thin). Paper helps absorb moisture to keep rounds crisp. Microwave on **HIGH (100%) 45 SECONDS**. Have 2 more plates ready to pop in the microwave at 45 seconds each. Serve hot.

JALAPEÑO CHEESE PIE

antijito de queso y jalapeño

Cooking Time: 6 minutes
Utensils: 1½-quart glass ring mold dish
Servings: 6–8 or more

**1/2 cup jalapeño peppers,
  seeded and sliced
1 (10-oz.) package Longhorn
  Cheddar cheese, (4 cups
  grated)**

1. Place seeded and sliced peppers on paper towels to drain. Line bottom of greased 1½-quart ring mold with peppers. Spread grated cheese over peppers.

4 eggs

2. Beat eggs until foamy and pour over cheese. Microwave on **HIGH (100%) 6 MINUTES**, rotating dish at 2-minute intervals. Let stand 5 minutes before slicing into wedges or bite-size servings.

HOT CRAB PUFFS

pasta frolla con granchi

Cooking Time: 1 minute per plate of 12
Utensils: Paper plates or several glass plates
Servings: 100 puffs

**1 pound white crabmeat
2 cups mayonnaise
Juice of small lemon
1/4 teaspoon salt
1/4 teaspoon red pepper
3 egg whites**

1. Combine crabmeat with mayonnaise. Add lemon juice, salt and pepper. Beat egg whites until stiff and fold into crab mixture.

Triscuits or melba rounds

2. Place one heaping teaspoon of crab mixture on each Triscuit. Arrange 12 on a plate. Microwave on **HIGH (100%) 1 MINUTE** per plate as needed. Serve warm.

MEXICAN CHILI PEANUTS

cacahuates mexicanos
Pronounced cah-cah-OO-wah-tēz

Cooking Time: 5 minutes 45 seconds
Utensil: 9-inch browning dish with lid
Servings: "Never enough"

1 teaspoon vegetable oil
15 small whole cloves of garlic, peeled*
1½ cups large roasted, salted peanuts without skins (not dry roasted)

1. Preheat empty browning dish on **HIGH (100%) 4 MINUTES**. Add oil, whole garlic cloves and peanuts, stirring quickly so garlic and peanuts will "roast" and not burn. Cover and microwave on **HIGH (100%) 1 MINUTE**.

1 Tablespoon Gebhardt's chili powder

2. Add chili powder. Stir to coat peanuts and garlic. Cover and microwave on **HIGH (100%) 45 SECONDS**. Remove quickly to a serving plate. Let stand 10 minutes to crisp peanuts before serving. When cool, keep crisp in a tightly closed jar.

"The garlic cloves are delicious, too."

***MICRO MEMO** for peeling garlic in the food processor:

Using the steel blade and the machine running, drop all the garlic cloves in the feeder tube. When the blade hits the garlic cloves, the skin will be loosened on some and removed on others. Process only a moment.

MEXICAN DIP
salsa mexicana

Cooking Time: 30 seconds
Utensil: 1-quart glass mixing bowl
Servings: Makes about 2 cups

1 large bunch green onions, tops and bulbs, chopped
1 large ripe tomato, chopped
1 (4-oz.) can whole green chilies, seeded and chopped
Juice of one lemon
2 teaspoons McCormick seasoned salt

Mix together green onions, tomato and green chilies. Place whole lemon in microwave on **HIGH (100%) 30 SECONDS** (for easier squeezing). Add lemon juice and seasoned salt to taste. Use as a dip with corn chips or tortillas. Also good as a side dish with Mexican dishes and all vegetables.

TAMALE DIP
tamales para sopear

Cooking Time: 8 minutes
Utensils: 1-cup glass measuring cup
         2-quart glass dish
Servings: Makes 2 quarts

2 (14½-oz.) cans tamales

1. Remove wrappers from tamales. Chop coarsely in food processor with steel blade.

1 large onion (1 cup), minced

2. In a 1-cup measure cover onion with plastic wrap and microwave on **HIGH (100%) 2 MINUTES**.

1 (15-oz.) can chile con carne
1 pound Cheddar cheese, grated

3. Place chopped tamales in a 2-quart dish. Add onion, chile con carne and cheese. Microwave on **HIGH (100%) 6 MINUTES** until cheese melts. Stir at 3 minutes. Serve with tostadas.

MUSHROOMS YARBROUGH

champignons yarbrough

Magnifique!

Cooking Time: 6 minutes
Utensils: 1-quart glass measuring cup
9-inch glass pie plate
Servings: 6

8 ounces large fresh mushrooms
1/4 cup unsalted butter*
4 large green onions, with bulbs and tops finely chopped separately
1/2 teaspoon garlic salt
1/4 teaspoon dry mustard

1. Rinse mushrooms and remove stems. Chop half the stems finely. Micromelt butter in a 1-quart bowl or measure, add and sauté chopped stems, green onion bulbs, garlic salt and dry mustard on **HIGH (100%) 2 MINUTES**.

1 teaspoon soy sauce
1/8 teaspoon oregano
1½ Tablespoons Parmesan cheese, grated
1½ Tablespoons Romano cheese, grated
3 Tablespoons Italian seasoned bread crumbs
Grated Parmesan and Romano cheese for sprinkling

2. Stir in soy sauce, oregano, chopped green onion tops, cheese and bread crumbs. Microwave on **HIGH (100%) 1 MINUTE**. Stuff mushroom caps with mixture and place in a buttered 9-inch pie plate. Sprinkle grated Parmesan and Romano cheese over mushrooms. Cover with plastic wrap. When ready to serve, microwave on **HIGH (100%) 3 MINUTES**. Rotate dish 1 time.

*MICRO MEMO:
 If margarine is used, substitute garlic powder for garlic salt.

SAUSAGE STUFFED MUSHROOMS

champignons farcis

Cooking Time: 9 minutes 30 seconds
Utensils: 4-cup glass measuring cup
          2 (12-inch) glass plates
Servings: 24 mushrooms

**24 large mushrooms
2 Tablespoons margarine
2 cloves garlic, crushed
8 ounces Owens bulk pork
    sausage (4-oz. hot and
    4-oz. mild)
1/4 teaspoon thyme
1/4 teaspoon basil
1/4 teaspoon savory
1/4 teaspoon salt
1/8 teaspoon red pepper
2 Tablespoons seasoned
    bread crumbs
1/4 cup Mozzarella cheese,
    grated
2 Tablespoons snipped
    parsley**

1. Rinse mushrooms, remove stems from caps and chop, reserving caps. Micromelt margarine in a 4-cup measure on **HIGH (100%) 30 SECONDS**. Add mushroom stems, garlic, and sausage and cover with wax paper. Microwave on **HIGH (100%) 5 MINUTES**. Stir one time. Drain off fat. Stir in thyme, basil, savory, salt, red pepper, bread crumbs, cheese and parsley. Mound into mushroom caps.

**1/4 cup melted margarine
2 Tablespoons white wine or
    Vermouth
Parsley for garnish**

2. Place mushrooms on 2 large glass plates with larger caps on outer edge of plate. Brush each with melted margarine. Pour 1 tablespoon wine in center of each dish. Cover with plastic wrap and microwave each dish on **HIGH (100%) 2 MINUTES**, rotating dish 1 time. Serve warm, garnished with parsley.
Compliments of Joe Broussard.

SHRIMP CAROL

A dip or entrée.

Cooking Time: 18 minutes
Utensils: 1½-quart glass casserole dish
8-cup glass measuring cup
Servings: Makes 2 quarts

2 pounds shrimp, shelled
4 cloves garlic, crushed
1 teaspoon Creole seasoning
  (or your favorite
  seasoning)
Juice of 1 lemon
1/2 teaspoon salt
1/4 cup dry Vermouth

1. Place shelled shrimp and garlic in a 1½-quart dish. Sprinkle on seasoning. Cover and microwave on **HIGH (100%) 6 MINUTES** stirring at 3 minutes. Add lemon juice (with salt dissolved) and Vermouth. Cover and microwave on **HIGH (100%) 1 to 2 MINUTES** until all shrimp are pink; do not overcook. Let stand in liquid and cover while proceeding to step 2.

1/4 cup margarine
1 cup onions, chopped
1 cup green bell pepper,
  chopped
2/3 cup celery, chopped
4 Tablespoons flour
1½ cups heavy cream
1 pound Velveeta cheese,
  cubed
3 Tablespoons tomato paste

2. In an 8-cup measure micro-melt margarine on **HIGH (100%) 1 MINUTE**. Add onion, bell pepper and celery. Sauté on **HIGH (100%) 6 MINUTES**. Stir in flour and add cream slowly. Microwave on **HIGH (100%) 3 MINUTES**, stirring once, until mixture thickens. Stir cheese into hot mixture until melted. Add tomato paste.

1/4 teaspoon white pepper
Salt (if needed)
Melba Rounds or pastry
  shells

3. Drain shrimp and add to cheese sauce along with white pepper. Taste for salt. Serve with Melba Rounds or in pastry shells.

SHRIMP AND MUSHROOMS
gamberetti e funghi

Cooking Time: 9 minutes
Utensils: 2-quart glass dish
Servings: 6–8

1/4 cup margarine
3 cloves garlic, minced
1 Tablespoon parsley,
**   chopped**
1/4 cup Vermouth or white
**   wine**
3 Tablespoons lemon juice
1 teaspoon salt
1/2 teaspoon ground pepper
2 cups whole fresh
**   mushrooms**

1 pound medium large
**   shrimp, peeled**

1. Melt margarine in a 2-quart dish on **HIGH (100%) 1 MINUTE**. Stir in garlic, parsley, wine, lemon juice, salt and pepper. Add mushrooms and mix well. Microwave on **HIGH (100%) 3 MINUTES**.

2. Add shrimp. Cover. Microwave on **HIGH (100%) 5 MINUTES** until all shrimp are pink. Stir shrimp after half the cooking time. Let stand in sauce. When ready to serve, use a slotted spoon to remove shrimp and mushrooms to a serving dish. Sauce may be used as a dip for the shrimp and mushrooms. Serve with wooden picks.

SMOKED COCKTAIL SAUSAGE
salsiccie affumicate

Cooking Time: 9 minutes
Utensil: 1½ or 2-quart glass casserole
Servings: 20

1 pound miniature smoked cocktail sausages (about 50) or 1 pound smoked link sausage, cut in bite-size rounds, may be substituted

1. Add smoked sausage to hot sauce* in a 1½ or 2-quart dish. Let sit in sauce until serving time. Just before serving, warm on **HIGH (100%) 4 MINUTES** until heated through, stirring once.
2. After heating, place sausage and sauce in chafing dish stand over low flame during party.

*Sauce for Smoked Sausage

2 Tablespoons instant dry minced onion
1 Tablespoon brown sugar
2 teaspoons dry mustard
1/2 cup water
1/4 cup olive oil
1 cup catsup
2 Tablespoons tarragon vinegar
2 Tablespoons red wine vinegar

2 Tablespoons Worcestershire sauce
3 drops commercial Liquid Smoke
1 Tablespoon chili powder
2 teaspoons paprika
1 teaspoon salt
1 teaspoon black pepper
1 teaspoon oregano
1 clove garlic, crushed
1 bay leaf

Combine all ingredients for sauce in a 1½ or 2-quart serving dish. Microwave on **HIGH (100%) 5 MINUTES** until sauce begins to bubble.

Gumbo
Soup

Gumbo:

Gumbo can be made with or without a roux. Compare Seafood Gumbo II, without a roux to Seafood Gumbo in Tout de Suite I *on page 36 with a roux.*

Soup: *sopa   Spanish*
          zuppa   Italian
               potages   French

Soup is a natural "instant meal" waiting for the dip of the spoon.

SEAFOOD GUMBO II

gumbo aux fruits de mer

Cooking Time: 1 hour 30 minutes
Utensils: 4 and 5-quart casseroles
Servings: 8

**Fresh shrimp heads and/or
  shells and/or fresh fish
  bones**
1½ quarts water
**3 celery stalks, cut into 2-
  inch pieces**
1 medium onion, quartered
2 cloves garlic, crushed
1/2 lemon, quartered

1. To make seafood stock,* combine shells, bones, water, celery, onion, garlic and lemon in a 4-quart casserole. Microwave on **HIGH (100%) 30 MINUTES.** Let stand until needed, then strain.

1 teaspoon vegetable oil
1½ cups onion, diced
**1 cup green bell pepper,
  diced**
**1 (16-oz.) can whole
  tomatoes, drained and
  chopped**
1/2 cup tomato purée
1½ quarts seafood stock*
8 crab claws

2. Sauté oil, onion and green pepper in a 5-quart covered casserole on **HIGH (100%) 8 MINUTES** until softened. Add tomatoes, tomato purée, stock and crab claws. Cover. Bring to a boil on **HIGH (100%) about 16 MINUTES.**

**1 (10-oz.) carton frozen cut
  okra**
1½ teaspoons gumbo filé
**1 Tablespoon Creole
  seasoning**
3/4 teaspoon garlic powder
3/4 teaspoon thyme
1/2 teaspoon saffron
2 bay leaves
2 teaspoons salt
**1–1½ pounds raw shrimp,
  peeled**
12 raw oysters and liquid
1 pound lump crabmeat

3. Microwave carton of okra on **HIGH (100%) 6 MINUTES.** Add okra to gumbo along with filé, Creole seasoning, garlic powder, thyme, saffron, bay leaves and salt. Microwave covered on **HIGH (100%) 10 MINUTES.** Add shrimp, oysters and crabmeat. Cover. Microwave on **MEDIUM (50%) 20 MINUTES** or until shrimp are tender and pink, stirring once or twice. Serve in gumbo bowls with steamed rice.

TURKEY GUMBO

Cooking Time: Roux 12 minutes
Gumbo 30 minutes
Utensils: 4-cup Pyrex glass measuring cup
5-quart ceramic casserole
Servings: 8

2/3 cup flour
2/3 cup vegetable oil } Roux

2 cups onions, chopped
1 cup celery, chopped
1/2 cup green bell pepper, chopped
4 cloves garlic, minced
1/4 cup parsley, chopped
1/4 cup green onion tops, chopped

2 (10-oz.) cartons frozen cut okra, cooked
1 (1-lb.) can tomatoes, drained and chopped
3 cups turkey stock
5 cups warm water
1 Tablespoon salt
1/2 teaspoon black pepper
1/4 teaspoon red pepper
2 teaspoons Worcestershire sauce
1 teaspoon Tabasco
3–4 cups cooked turkey, cubed

1. Mix flour and oil together in a 4-cup Pyrex measuring cup. Microwave on **HIGH (100%) 6–7 MINUTES**. Stir at 6 minutes. Roux will be a light brown color at this time and will need to cook 30 to 60 seconds longer to reach a dark brown color.

2. Add onion, celery and bell pepper to Roux in measuring cup. Stir and microwave on **HIGH (100%) 3 MINUTES**. Add garlic, parsley and green onion to Roux, stir and microwave on **HIGH (100%) 2 MINUTES**. Stir and pour Roux into a 5-quart casserole.

3. Remove outer wrapper and place both cartons of okra on a plate. Microwave on **HIGH (100%) 10 MINUTES**. Stir cooked okra into Roux. Add tomatoes, stock, water, salt, pepper, Worcestershire and Tabasco. Cover and microwave on **HIGH (100%) 10 MINUTES**.

4. Add turkey and check seasoning. Cover and microwave on **HIGH (100%) 10 MINUTES**. Serve with steamed rice. Gumbo may be frozen.

THE BIG POT GUMBO

Cooked in a pot bigger than your kitchen

FOR ONE 325 GALLON GUMBO

First you make a 12 gallon Roux, then you drink a Beer
— add—
1000 pounds chicken
200 pounds fryer gizzards
100 pounds smoked sausage
600 dozen oyster
300 pounds onions
75 pounds bell peppers
30 bunch celery
60 heads of garlic
12 gallons roux
3 pounds red pepper
½ gallon tabasco
then you drink two Beers
1 pound black pepper
8 pounds salt
50 bunch parsley
100 bunch of green onions
5 gallons cooking oil
— and —
300 pounds cooked rice
then you drink all the Beer!

Compliments of Big Mac McJimsey

SPANISH AVOCADO SOUP

sopa de aguacate a la española

Cooking Time: 18 minutes 30 seconds
Utensils: 8-cup glass measuring cup
          2-quart serving dish
Servings: 6–8

2 Tablespoons margarine
1 cup onion, chopped
7 large garlic cloves, peeled
2 (14½-oz.) cans clear chicken broth, undiluted

1. Micromelt margarine in an 8-cup measure on **HIGH (100%) 30 SECONDS**. Add onion and whole garlic. Sauté on **HIGH (100%) 3 MINUTES**. Add chicken broth. Cover and microwave on **HIGH (100%) 8 MINUTES**. Stir and continue to cook covered on **HIGH (100%) 7 MINUTES**. Let cool slightly.

1 large ripe avocado, peeled, seeded and chopped
Juice of 1/2 lime
1½ cups buttermilk
1 teaspoon salt
1/2 teaspoon white pepper
Minced green onion tops (garnish)

2. Purée mixture in batches in blender. Transfer to serving dish. Purée avocado and lime juice and add to broth. Blend in buttermilk, season with salt and pepper. Garnish with green onion tops and serve hot or cold.

CAULIFLOWER SOUP

soupe chou-fleur

Cooking Time: 21 minutes
Utensils: Paper plate
            3-quart casserole
Servings: Makes 8 cups

**1 medium head cauliflower
(1½–2 pounds)**

1. Rinse, then place whole cauliflower on a small paper plate. Cover cauliflower and plate with plastic wrap. Microwave on **HIGH (100%) 4 MINUTES**. Turn cauliflower package over and continue to cook on **HIGH (100%) 4 MINUTES**. Keep covered while preparing the next step.

**1 cup onion, chopped
1/2 cup celery, chopped
3½ cups chicken stock or 2
(13¾-oz.) cans chicken
broth
1/2 cup water
1 teaspoon salt
1 teaspoon celery salt
1/4 teaspoon white pepper
1 teaspoon Worcestershire
sauce**

2. Wilt onion and celery in a 3-quart casserole covered with plastic wrap on **HIGH (100%) 3 MINUTES**. Add chicken stock, water, salt, celery salt, white pepper and Worcestershire sauce. Cut cauliflower in flowerets and add to liquid. Cover and microwave on **HIGH (100%) 8 MINUTES**. Pour a small amount of hot mixture into blender and purée until all is blended. Return soup to the 3-quart casserole.

**1½ cups light cream or
evaporated milk**

3. Stir in light cream and microwave on **HIGH (100%) 2 MINUTES** or until hot.

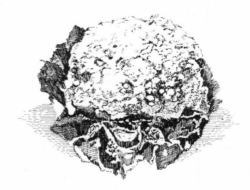

CHEDDAR CHEESE SOUP
minestra di formaggio

Cooking Time: 28 minutes 30 seconds
Utensils: Paper plate
        2-cup and 4-cup glass measuring cups
        4 or 5-quart glass or ceramic casserole
Servings: 8

1 small head cauliflower

1. Rinse and place cauliflower on a small paper plate. Cover with plastic wrap. Microwave on **HIGH (100%) 3 MINUTES**. Turn cauliflower package over and microwave on **HIGH (100%) 4 MINUTES 30 SECONDS**. Dice and measure 3/4 cup.

2 Tablespoons margarine
1/2 cup finely chopped
    carrots
1 cup finely chopped onions
1 cup mushrooms, sliced
2 Tablespoons cornstarch

2. Melt margarine in a 4-cup measure on **HIGH (100%) 1 MINUTE**. Add carrots and onions. Cover with plastic wrap. Sauté on **HIGH (100%) 3 MINUTES**. Stir in mushrooms and the 3/4 cup diced cauliflower. Microwave covered on **HIGH (100%) 3 MINUTES**. Stir in cornstarch. Set aside covered.

2 cups water
1 pound medium-sharp
    Cheddar cheese,
    shredded

3. Bring water to a boil in a 2-cup measure on **HIGH (100%) 5 MINUTES**. Place cheese in a 4 or 5-quart casserole and slowly pour and stir boiling water over cheese to melt. Microwave on **MEDIUM (50%) 5 MINUTES**. Continue to stir until cheese melts. Cheese will smooth out as other ingredients are added.

1 teaspoon salt
1/4 teaspoon red pepper
1 teaspoon Worcestershire
    sauce
Dash garlic powder
3/4 cup Canadian bacon,
    diced
2 cups half and half cream

4. Add salt, pepper, Worcestershire sauce and garlic powder. Stir in sautéed vegetables along with Canadian bacon. Cover and microwave on **HIGH (100%) 4 MINUTES**. Add half and half cream until desired thickness is reached.

CHICKEN AND CORN SOUP
sopa de pollo y maíz

Cooking Time: Chicken 40 minutes
Soup 33 minutes
Utensils: 5-quart ceramic casserole
2-cup glass measuring cup
Servings: Makes 4 quarts

2 (2½-lb) chickens, cut in pieces
6 cups water and 2 teaspoons salt
1/4 cup white wine
1 onion sliced
1 stalk celery with leaves
1/4 teaspoon pepper
1 bay leaf

1 cup celery, coarsely chopped and wilted

6 cups hot chicken stock
1½ cups uncooked medium egg noodles
1 (16-oz.) can cream style corn
2 Tablespoons fresh parsley, snipped
1 teaspoon celery salt
1½ teaspoon salt
1/4 teaspoon red pepper
1/2 teaspoon white pepper

1. In a 5-quart casserole combine chicken, salted water, wine, onion, celery, pepper and bay leaf. Cover and microwave on **HIGH (100%) 40 MINUTES** or until tender. Reserve 6 cups of chicken stock. Bone chicken and cut into bite-size pieces (approximately 4 cups). Set aside.

2. Place celery in a 2-cup measure, cover with plastic wrap and microwave on **HIGH (100%) 4 MINUTES**.

3. Bring stock to boil in a 5-quart casserole on **HIGH (100%), approximately 12 MINUTES**. Add wilted celery, noodles, corn, parsley, celery salt, salt and pepper. Cover. Microwave on **HIGH (100%) 12 MINUTES** stirring 2 times. Add cooked chicken, cover and microwave on **HIGH (100%) 5 MINUTES**.

SHRIMP BISQUE

A blend of shrimp, onions and potatoes.

Cooking Time: 5–6 minutes
Utensil: 8-cup glass measuring cup
Servings: 4 (6-oz.) servings

Follow directions for Cajun Shrimp Bake on page 59. Serve part of the recipe as suggested, reserving remaining shrimp, onions, potatoes and stock to make a quick bisque.

2 cups shrimp, cooked
2 new potatoes, cooked
1/2 onion, cooked
Stock from cooked shrimp
1–1½ cups half and half
** cream**
1/2 teaspoon garlic salt
1/4 teaspoon Tabasco sauce

1. Peel shrimp and potatoes. Reserve 4 shrimp for garnish. Purée shrimp, potatoes and onion in blender or food processor, adding stock to blend. Add half and half cream, garlic salt and Tabasco, blending well.

2 teaspoons butter, cut in 4
** pieces**

2. Pour mixture into an 8-cup measure and microwave on **HIGH (100%) 5–6 MINUTES** or until heated through. Stir at 1 minute intervals. Serve in bowls with a pat of butter on top and a shrimp for garnish.

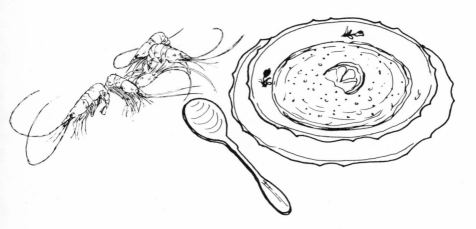

SPAGHETTINI AU GRATIN

Cooking Time: 13 minutes
Utensils: 5-quart ceramic casserole
Servings: 8

3/4 cup olive oil
2 cups green onions, tops
   and bulbs, chopped
2 Tablespoons salt
1 teaspoon pepper
10 cups boiling water

10 ounces Spaghettini (a
   very thin spaghetti)
1 cup parsley, minced
5 ounces Romano cheese,
   grated

6 large eggs

1. Heat olive oil in a 5-quart casserole on **HIGH (100%) 5 MINUTES**. Add green onions. Cover and micro-wave on **HIGH (100%) 3 MINUTES**. Add salt, pepper and 10 cups (2½ quarts) boiling water.

2. Stir pasta into boiling mixture. Microwave on **HIGH (100%) 4 MIN-UTES** until *al dente* (to the bite or the dent, tender but firm), stirring twice. Add parsley and cheese.

3. Stir eggs very slightly with a fork, just enough to pierce the yolks for a gentle blending with whites. Pour eggs very slowly into hot mixture stirring continuously with a large fork. Microwave on **HIGH (100%) 1 MINUTE**, being careful not to over-cook the pasta. Serve in individual bowls with freshly ground pepper.

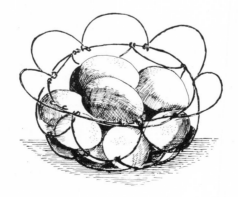

CRÈME DE TOMATE DUBARRY
With crème fraîche

Cooking Time: 30–33 minutes
Utensils: 5-quart Corning casserole
        1-cup glass measuring cup
Servings: 10–12

Prepare crème fraîche the day before. See page 43.

**3 large carrots, peeled and
  sliced in thin rounds**
3 large onions, sliced
**6 cups chicken stock, fresh or
  canned**
**6½ cups (approximately 2½
  pounds) ripe tomatoes,
  peeled and seeded**
2 strips lemon peel
1 teaspoon salt
1/4 teaspoon white pepper
**Pinch of laurier (powdered
  bay leaf)**
3 Tablespoons sugar

4 Tablespoons butter
4 Tablespoons cornstarch
2 cups crème fraîche

**Zest of 3 oranges (grated
  rind)**
1/2 cup water

1. Place carrots and onions in a 5-quart dish. Cover with plastic wrap and microwave on **HIGH (100%) 7 MINUTES** or until carrots and onions are softened. Add chicken stock, tomatoes, lemon peel, salt, pepper, laurier and sugar. Cover and bring to a boil on **HIGH (100%) 12–15 MINUTES**, stirring once.

2. Add butter. Mix small amount of hot soup into cornstarch. Add to soup to thicken. Continue to cook covered on **HIGH (100%) 9 MINUTES**. Strain soup through a colander and purée only the vegetables in a blender. Return soup and puréed vegetables to the 5-quart casserole. Add crème fraîche and reheat before serving.

3. In a 1-cup measure add orange zest and water. Cook on **HIGH (100%) 2 MINUTES** to blanch the zest. (This is to remove citrus tang.) Drain and pass zest separately to sprinkle on top of soup. The blanched orange zest makes this soup extraordinary! **DO NOT OMIT!**

TORTILLA SOUP

sopa de tortilla

Cooking Time: 22 minutes
Utensil: 3-quart ceramic casserole
Servings: 8

1 cup onion, chopped
1 clove garlic, chopped
5 cups chicken stock, fresh or canned
1 (1-lb. 12-oz.) can whole tomatoes, drained and chopped (about 2 cups)
1 jalapeño pepper, seeded and quartered
2 teaspoons cumin
1 teaspoon chili powder
1½ teaspoons salt
1/8 teaspoon pepper

1. Sauté onion, garlic and 2 tablespoons of chicken stock in a 3-quart casserole on **HIGH (100%) 5 MINUTES** until limp. Add remaining stock, tomatoes, jalapeño pepper, cumin, chili powder, salt and pepper. Bring mixture to a boil on **HIGH (100%) 12 MINUTES**.

6 tortillas, cut in 1-inch squares (old, dry tortillas are best in this soup)
1/2 cup Monterey Jack cheese, grated
1/2 cup Cheddar cheese, grated
8 slices jalapeño pepper

2. Add tortilla pieces to soup and continue to microwave on **HIGH (100%) 5 MINUTES**. Let stand 10 minutes. Ladle soup into bowls. Top each serving with spoonfuls of Monterey Jack and Cheddar cheese and a slice of jalapeño pepper. For extra flavor, pieces of chopped chicken may be added.

VICHYSSOISE
With crème fraîche

Cooking Time: 15 minutes
Utensil: 2-quart glass dish
Servings: 6–8

3 large leeks
3 medium Irish potatoes,
peeled
1 teaspoon butter

1. Slice the white part of leeks and quarter the potatoes. Place in a 2-quart dish, dot with butter and cover with plastic wrap. Microwave on **HIGH (100%) 10 MINUTES**, stirring one time.

1 quart chicken stock, fresh
or canned
1/2 cup white wine
1 teaspoon salt
1/2 teaspoon celery salt
1/2 teaspoon white pepper
1 cup crème fraîche* or 1 cup
whipped cream
chopped chives

2. Add stock, wine, salt, celery salt and pepper to potatoes and leeks. Microwave on **HIGH (100%) 5 MINUTES**. Strain through a colander and purée leeks and potatoes. Return puréed mixture to liquid and add 1 cup of crème fraîche.* Chill; garnish with chives.

* Crème Fraîche:

To prepare 2 cups of crème fraîche *(pronounced crème fresh), mix 2 cups of whipping cream and 2 Tablespoons of buttermilk together in a jar or 4-cup measure. Cover with plastic wrap and Microwave* **10 MINUTES on DEFROST** *to bring mixture to room temperature. Place container in a warm spot for 18 to 24 hours. Stir once or twice. Refrigerate several hours until thick. Crème fraîche may also be used as a topping for fruit or in cake icings. For a "slim" crème fraîche substitute half and half for whipping cream.*

Fish

Shellfish

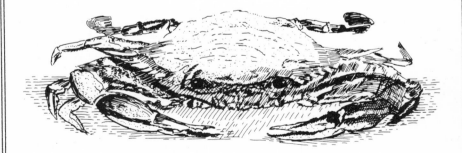

Fish:
pescado   Spanish
pesci   Italian
poissons   French

Shellfish:
comidas del mar   Spanish
frutti di mare   Italian
fruits de mer   French

Fish and shellfish are universal to all cultures, from the simplest menu to the most extravagant.

FLOUNDER FILLETS WITH CRABMEAT

filets de flounder au chair de crabe

Cooking Time: 7 minutes
Utensils: 7 x 11-inch glass baking dish
         1-quart glass bowl
Servings: 6

1½ to 2 pounds flounder fillets (red snapper, red fish or trout fillets may be substituted)

1. Thaw fish if frozen, cut into 6 serving pieces and dry on paper towels before placing in a 7 x 11-inch glass baking dish.

1 Tablespoon margarine
3 Tablespoons onion, minced
3 Tablespoons parsley, minced
3 Tablespoons green onion tops, chopped

2. Sauté margarine, onion, parsley and green onion tops in a 1-quart bowl on **HIGH (100%) 2 MINUTES**.

1/2 pound crabmeat
1/4 cup seasoned bread crumbs
1/2 teaspoon salt
1/2 teaspoon white pepper
1/2 teaspoon cayenne pepper
1 egg white beaten with
2 Tablespoons milk

3. Stir in crabmeat, bread crumbs, salt, pepper, cayenne pepper, egg white and milk. Spread crabmeat mixture over fillets in baking dish. Cover with wax paper. Microwave on **HIGH (100%) 5 MINUTES** or until fish flakes easily with a fork. Turn dish once. Garnish with parsley and lemon slices.

TROUT AMANDINE

Trout with almonds

Cooking Time: 9 minutes 30 seconds
Utensils: 8 x 8-inch glass dish
             2-cup glass measuring cup
Servings: 6

**2 pounds trout fillets or
   other fish fillets, fresh or
   frozen
Red pepper for sprinkling
2 Tablespoons margarine,
   melted**

1. Defrost fish if frozen. Cut fillets into serving size portions. Drain on paper towels. Sprinkle fillets lightly with red pepper and place in an 8 x 8-inch shallow dish. Drizzle with margarine. Cover and microwave on **HIGH (100%) 5 MINUTES**, rotate dish 1 time. Fish should flake easily with a fork when done. Drain excess liquid off.

**2 Tablespoons margarine
1/2 cup sliced almonds
2 Tablespoons lemon juice
1 Tablespoon parsley,
   chopped
1/2 teaspoon salt
1/8 teaspoon Tabasco sauce
Parsley sprigs for garnish**

2. In a 2-cup measure melt margarine on **HIGH (100%) 30 SECONDS**. Add almonds and microwave on **HIGH (100%) 2 MINUTES**. Stir in lemon juice, parsley, salt and Tabasco. Pour sauce over fish. Cover. Just before serving microwave covered on **HIGH (100%) 2 MINUTES** to reheat. Garnish with parsley.

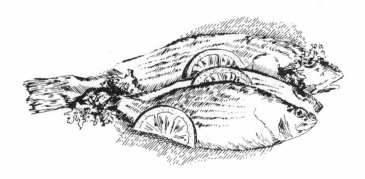

47

FILLET OF RED SNAPPER WITH SHRIMP

filets de red snapper aux crevettes

In Veracruz Sauce

Cooking Time: 14 minutes
Utensils: 1-quart glass dish
4-cup glass measuring cup
2-quart shallow glass baking dish
Servings: 6

2 pounds red snapper fillets

1. Thaw and drain fish on paper towels and set aside while preparing sauce.

1 cup shrimp, shelled
Cayenne pepper
1 slice onion
1 slice lemon

2. Place shrimp in a 1-quart dish. Sprinkle with cayenne pepper and add a slice of onion and lemon. Cover. Microwave on **HIGH (100%) 3–4 MINUTES** until all shrimp are pink. Stir once. Drain.

VERACRUZ SAUCE:

4 Tablespoons margarine
1/2 cup onion, chopped
1/2 cup green bell pepper, chopped
1 clove garlic, minced
1 (4-oz.) can mushrooms, drained and sliced
1 small tomato, peeled, seeded and chopped
3 Tablespoons chili sauce
2 Tablespoons lemon juice
2 Tablespoons capers, drained
1 Tablespoon parsley, snipped
1½ teaspoons thyme
1/2 teaspoon salt
2 Tablespoons dry white wine

3. Micromelt margarine in a 4-cup measure on **HIGH (100%) 1 MINUTE**. Add onion, bell pepper and garlic and sauté on **HIGH (100%) 3 MINUTES**. Add mushrooms, tomato, chili sauce, lemon juice, capers, parsley, thyme and salt. Stir in shrimp and wine. Pour sauce into a shallow 2-quart greased dish. Place thawed fish on top. Spoon some of the sauce over fish. Cover and microwave on **HIGH (100%) 5–6 MINUTES** until fish flakes easily with a fork.

RED SNAPPER FILLETS

With Indies Isle sauce

Cooking Time: 8 minutes
Utensils: Shallow 2-quart glass or ceramic dish
2-cup glass measuring cup
Servings: 6

2 pounds red snapper fillets (flounder or trout may be substituted)

1. Completely thaw and drain fish on paper towels before placing in a shallow 2-quart baking dish.

INDIES ISLE SAUCE:

1/4 cup margarine
1/2 pound fresh mushrooms, sliced
1/4 cup green onion tops, chopped
1 Tablespoon parsley, snipped
2 teaspoons lime juice
1/2 teaspoon garlic powder
1/2 teaspoon salt
1/4 teaspoon cayenne pepper

2. Micromelt margarine in a 2-cup measure on **HIGH (100%) 1 MINUTE**. Add mushrooms, onions, parsley, lime juice, garlic powder, salt and cayenne pepper. Stir to mix. Microwave sauce on **HIGH (100%) 1 MINUTE**.

Parsley and lime slices for garnish

3. Pour sauce over fillets in baking dish. Cover with wax paper. Microwave on **HIGH (100%) 5 to 6 MINUTES**, or until fish flakes easily with a fork. Rotate dish once. Garnish with parsley and lime slices.

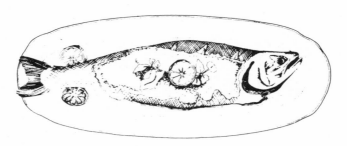

RED SNAPPER PICANTE

huachinango picante

Cooking Time: 11 minutes
Utensils: 7 x 11-inch glass baking dish
         4-cup glass measuring cup
Servings: 6

**2 pounds red snapper fillets,
  completely thawed
1 Tablespoon lime juice**

1. Drain fillets on paper towels. Prick surface of fillets with fork and arrange in a 7 x 11-inch baking dish. Sprinkle fillets with lime juice. Cover while preparing sauce.

SALSA PICANTE:

**1 Tablespoon olive oil
1 small onion, sliced thin
1 large clove garlic, sliced
1 (8-oz.) can tomato sauce
1/2 cup commercial Picante
  sauce
1 bay leaf
2 Tablespoons jalapeño
  pepper strips in
  Escabeche (canned)
8 pimiento-stuffed green
  olives, cut in half
1 Tablespoon capers
1/4 teaspoon salt
1/8 teaspoon oregano**

2. Mix olive oil, onion and garlic in a 4-cup measure. Microwave on **HIGH (100%) 3 MINUTES**. Add tomato sauce, Picante sauce, bay leaf, jalapeño pepper, olives, capers, salt, and oregano. Microwave on **HIGH (100%) 3 MINUTES**. Pour over fish, cover and microwave on **HIGH (100%) 5 MINUTES** or until fish flakes easily with a fork. Rotate dish once.

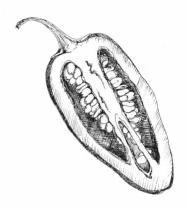

CRAB BAKED AVOCADOS

aguacates y cangrejo al horno

Cooking Time: 12 minutes
Utensils: 8-cup glass measuring cup
         2 (9-inch) round shallow baking dishes
Servings: 10–12

6 Tablespoons margarine
2 cups onions, chopped

1. Melt margarine on **HIGH (100%) 1 MINUTE** in an 8-cup measure. Add onions and sauté on **HIGH (100%) 5 MINUTES**.

1/2 cup heavy cream
1 teaspoon salt
1/4 teaspoon cayenne pepper
1/8 teaspoon paprika
1 pound white lump
**   crabmeat**
1/2 cup seasoned bread
**   crumbs**

2. Stir in cream, salt, pepper, paprika, crabmeat and bread crumbs. Cover with plastic wrap. Microwave on **HIGH (100%) 2 MINUTES**. Let stand covered until ready to stuff avocados.

5–6 ripe avocados, room
**   temperature**
Lemon slice
1 cup Cheddar cheese, finely
**   grated**
Parsley sprigs to garnish

3. Halve avocados, remove seeds, but do not peel. Rub lemon slice over avocado. Spoon crab mixture into avocados and sprinkle with cheese. Arrange 5 or 6 stuffed avocados in a circle in 2 shallow baking dishes. Microwave one dish on **HIGH (100%) 2 MINUTES**. Have the next dish ready to slip into the microwave on **HIGH (100%) 2 MINUTES**. Serve hot. Garnish with parsley. Stuffed halves may be microwaved in individual ramekins on **HIGH (100%) 30 SECONDS** each.

MICRO MEMO:

    To prepare avocado, halve lengthwise, then twist gently to separate. With fingers out of the way, whack a knife directly into seed and twist to lift out. To peel avocado, place cut side of avocado down and strip or pare the skin away.

CRAB ENCHILADAS

enchiladas de cangrejo

Cooking Time: 15 minutes
Utensils: 4-cup glass measuring cup
         7 x 11-inch glass baking dish
Servings: 6

SAUCE:

2 Tablespoons margarine
1 cup onion, chopped

1. In a 4-cup measure micromelt margarine on **HIGH (100%) 30 SECONDS**. Stir in onion and sauté on **HIGH (100%) 3 MINUTES**.

1 (10-oz.) can Ro-tel
   tomatoes and green
   chilies, chopped
1 (8-oz.) can tomato sauce
1 teaspoon chili powder
1/2 teaspoon oregano
1/2 teaspoon salt

2. Add tomatoes and green chilies, tomato sauce, chili powder, oregano and salt. Mix well. Bring to boil on **HIGH (100%) 2 MINUTES 30 SECONDS**. Cover with a paper towel and microwave on **HIGH (100%) 4 MINUTES** to blend flavors. Let stand covered.

FILLING:

1 pound white or claw
   crabmeat
2 cups Monterey Jack
   cheese, shredded and
   divided
1/3 cup chopped ripe olives

3. Combine crabmeat, 1 cup cheese, olives and 1/2 cup of sauce. Mix well.

TO ASSEMBLE:

12 soft corn tortillas
Dairy sour cream for topping

4. Dip each tortilla in warm sauce. Lay flat in greased 7 x 11-inch baking dish. Fill each tortilla with equal portions of crabmeat filling. Roll and place seam side down. Spoon remaining sauce over top and sprinkle with remaining 1 cup cheese. Microwave on **HIGH (100%) 5 MINUTES**. Rotate dish one time. Serve topped with sour cream, if desired.

CRABMEAT ACAPULCO

Cooking Time: 6 minutes
Utensils: 2-quart glass casserole dish
Servings: 6–8

1/2 cup margarine
1 cup onion, chopped

1. Micromelt margarine in a 2-quart casserole dish on **HIGH (100%) 1 MINUTE**. Add onion and sauté on **HIGH (100%) 3 MINUTES** until tender.

8 ounces cream cheese
1/2 teaspoon salt
1/4 teaspoon cayenne pepper
1/4 teaspoon white pepper
1/4 teaspoon Tabasco
1 pound white lump
**   crabmeat**
Triscuits or melba rounds or
**   pastry shells**

2. Add cream cheese, salt, pepper and Tabasco to sautéed onions. Stir until well blended. Fold crabmeat in gently. Microwave on **HIGH (100%) 2–3 MINUTES** until heated through. Serve warm with Triscuits, melba rounds or in pastry shells.

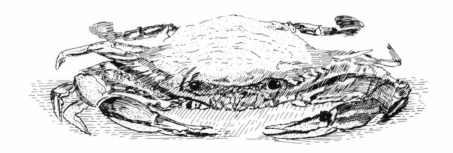

CRAWFISH AND CHICKEN SUPREME

écrevisses et volailles suprême

Cooking Time: 12 minutes 30 seconds
Utensils: 8-cup glass measuring cup
Servings: 8–10

1 (3-lb.) chicken, cut in pieces

1. Follow directions for "Cooked Chicken" on page 79. Dice cooked chicken and set aside. Reserve stock.

2 Tablespoons margarine
1 bunch green onions, tops and bulbs chopped
2 Tablespoons flour
1/2 cup evaporated milk
3/4 cup chicken stock

2. Micromelt margarine on **HIGH (100%) 30 SECONDS** in an 8-cup measure. Add green onions and sauté on **HIGH (100%) 3 MINUTES**. Stir in flour. Slowly add milk and stock. Microwave on **HIGH (100%) 4 MINUTES** until thickened. Stir 2 times.

6 ounces mild Cheddar cheese, grated
3 ounces Mozzarella cheese, grated
2 Tablespoons white wine
1 teaspoon salt
1/2 teaspoon cayenne pepper
1/4 teaspoon Tabasco
1/4 teaspoon garlic powder

3. Stir in cheese until melted. Add wine, salt, cayenne pepper, Tabasco, and garlic powder.

1 pound peeled crawfish tails (shrimp may be substituted)
Pastry shells for serving

4. Add diced cooked chicken and crawfish or shrimp, mixing well. Cover with wax paper. Microwave on **HIGH (100%) 5 MINUTES**, stirring once. Serve in pastry shells.

CRAWFISH ÉTOUFFÉE À LA ARCENEAUX

écrevisses étoufées à l'arceneaux

Cooking Time: 17 minutes
Utensil: 3-quart glass dish
Servings: 4

1/2 cup margarine
1½ cups onion, finely
    chopped
3/4 cup green bell pepper,
    finely chopped
1 clove garlic, minced or 1/4
    teaspoon garlic powder

1. Micromelt margarine in a 3-quart dish on **HIGH (100%) 1 MINUTE**. Add onion, bell pepper and garlic. Sauté on **HIGH (100%) 6 MINUTES** or until tender.

2 Tablespoons flour
2 heaping Tablespoons
    undiluted cream of
    celery soup
1 (10-oz.) can Ro-tel
    tomatoes and green
    chilies, puréed with
    liquid
1 cup beer
2 teaspoons salt
1 teaspoon cayenne pepper

2. Add flour and celery soup. Stir in puréed Ro-tel, beer, salt, and pepper. Microwave on **HIGH (100%) 6 MINUTES**.

1 pound peeled crawfish

3. Add crawfish. Cover. Microwave on **HIGH (100%) 4 MINUTES**. Serve étouffée over rice.

CRAWFISH RICE CASSEROLE

écrevisses et riz casserole

Cooking Time: 12 minutes
Utensil: 2-quart glass casserole
Servings: 6

1/4 cup margarine
1/2 cup onion, chopped
2/3 cup green bell pepper,
 chopped
1 cup celery, chopped
2 cloves garlic, minced

4 slices bread
1 (10½-oz.) can mushroom
 soup, undiluted
2 cups crawfish tails, peeled
 and seasoned with 1
 teaspoon Creole
 seasoning (or your
 favorite seasoning)
2 cups cooked rice
1 teaspoon parsley, snipped
1 teaspoon salt
1/4 teaspoon red pepper
Seasoned bread crumbs for
 topping

1. Micromelt margarine in a 2-quart dish on **HIGH (100%) 1 MINUTE**. Add onion, bell pepper, celery and garlic. Microwave on **HIGH (100%) 4 MINUTES**.

2. Moisten bread with water and break small pieces into the cooking dish. Add mushroom soup, crawfish, cooked rice, parsley, salt and red pepper and mix well. Top with seasoned bread crumbs. Microwave on **HIGH (100%) 7 MINUTES**.

HOLLANDAISE SAUCE

1/4 cup margarine
1 Tablespoon lemon juice
2 egg yolks, beaten
2 Tablespoons light cream
1/2 teaspoon dry mustard
1/4 teaspoon salt
Dash Tabasco sauce

Place margarine in a 2-cup glass measure. Microwave on **HIGH (100%) 1 MINUTE**. Stir in lemon juice, egg yolks, cream, mustard, salt and Tabasco. Microwave on **HIGH (100%) 1 MINUTE**, stirring every 15 seconds. Beat with wire whisk until smooth. Makes 2/3 cup.

OYSTERS REAGAN

huîtres reagan hollandaise

With Hollandaise Sauce

Cooking Time: 16 minutes 30 seconds
Utensils: Microsafe plate
        2 and 4-cup glass measuring cups
        12-inch round glass plate
        12 oyster or miniature shells
Servings: 4 (3 each)

1 (10-oz.) carton frozen chopped spinach

1. Remove outer waxed wrapper and place carton of spinach on plate. Microwave on **HIGH (100%) 7 MINUTES**. Drain. Set aside in carton.

12 raw oysters, drained
White pepper to sprinkle
Worcestershire sauce to season
1 egg, beaten
3/4 cup seasoned bread crumbs

2. Drain oysters and dry with paper towels. Season with white pepper and Worcestershire. Dip oysters in egg and roll in bread crumbs. Place on small plate and set aside.

1/3 cup onion, finely chopped
1 teaspoon margarine
1/2 teaspoon salt
1/4 teaspoon white pepper
Pinch nutmeg
2/3 cup Hollandaise Sauce
  (see page 56)

3. Sauté onion and margarine in a 4-cup measure on **HIGH (100%) 2 MINUTES**. Add cooked spinach, salt, white pepper and nutmeg. Heat thoroughly on **HIGH (100%) 3 MINUTES**. After preparing Hollandaise Sauce, cover oysters with wax paper and microwave on **HIGH (100%) 2 MINUTES. TO ASSEMBLE,** fill 12 shells with 1 tablespoon of spinach mixture and place on a 12-inch glass plate. Lay breaded oyster on hot spinach and coat each with Hollandaise Sauce. To warm just before serving, microwave on **HIGH (100%) 30–60 SECONDS**.

OYSTER AND SHRIMP JAMBALAYA

jambalaya d'huîtres et de crevettes

Cooking Time: 21 minutes
Utensils: 4-cup glass measuring cup
3-quart glass casserole
Servings: 8

1 cup raw rice or 3 to 4 cups cooked rice

1. Follow directions for cooking rice on page 133. Cover cooked rice and set aside.

3 Tablespoons oil
3 Tablespoons flour
1½ cups onion, chopped
1 clove garlic, minced
1 cup green bell pepper, chopped
1/4 cup celery, chopped
1/4 cup parsley, chopped

2. Stir oil and flour together until completely mixed in a 4-cup measure. Microwave on **HIGH (100%) 5 MINUTES** to make a light colored roux. Stir. Add onion, garlic, bell pepper, celery and parsley. Microwave on **HIGH (100%) 5 MINUTES** or until vegetables are soft.

1/4 teaspoon pepper
1/4 teaspoon red pepper
1½ pounds raw shrimp, peeled and deveined
3 dozen raw oysters
2 Tablespoons green onion tops, chopped
2½ teaspoons salt

3. Transfer mixture to a 3-quart casserole. Add pepper and shrimp. Microwave on **HIGH (100%) 6 MINUTES** until shrimp turn pink, stirring once or twice. Add oysters and microwave on **HIGH (100%) 2 MINUTES** just until edges of oysters curl. Add green onion tops, salt and 3 to 4 cups cooked rice, mixing together gently. Microwave on **HIGH (100%) 3 MINUTES**. Stir and let stand covered 10 minutes.

CAJUN SHRIMP BAKE

crevettes cajuns au four

Serve shrimp shelled or unshelled

Cooking Time: 20 minutes
Utensils: 2-quart glass or micro-plastic dish
         7 x 11-inch glass baking dish
Servings: 6

2 medium onions, cut in quarters or 8 miniature onions
8 small red potatoes, strip a 1/4-inch peeling around center of each
1 large green bell pepper, sliced in rings
1 Tablespoon water

1. Place onions, potatoes, bell pepper, and water in a 2-quart dish. Cover tightly and microwave on **HIGH (100%) 10 MINUTES**. Drain.

2 pounds large shrimp, headed and in shells
Cayenne pepper
Creole seasoning

2. Rinse, drain and, if desired, peel shrimp. Place in a 7 x 11-inch baking dish. Season liberally with cayenne pepper and Creole seasoning.

1/2 large lemon cut in thin circles
1/4 cup margarine
1 bay leaf
1 teaspoon salt

3. Spoon cooked vegetables over shrimp. Squeeze lemon juice over mixture and place circles of lemon rind on top. Dot with margarine and add bay leaf. Cover with plastic wrap and microwave on **HIGH (100%) 10 MINUTES**. Stir mixture after 5 minutes so shrimp will cook evenly. After cooking, sprinkle salt over shrimp and vegetables. Serve in shallow gumbo bowls with lots of French bread for dipping.

MICRO MEMO:

Try making Shrimp Bisque page 39 with leftovers!

CREOLE SHRIMP

crevettes créoles

First, you make a roux!

Cooking Time: 25 minutes
Utensils: 4-cup glass measuring cup
        3-quart glass or ceramic casserole
Servings: 8

2/3 cup oil   } **Roux**
2/3 cup flour

2 cups onion, chopped
1/4 cup celery, chopped

1 (10-oz.) can Ro-tel
    tomatoes and green
    chilies, chopped with
    liquid
1 (8-oz.) can tomato sauce
2 teaspoons salt
1/4 teaspoon red pepper
1/4 teaspoon garlic powder

2 pounds shrimp, peeled

1. Mix oil and flour together completely until smooth (no lumps) in a 4-cup glass measuring cup. Microwave uncovered on **HIGH (100%) 6 MINUTES**. Stir at 6 minutes and continue to microwave on **HIGH (100%) 30–60 SECONDS** longer to reach a dark brown color. Add onion and celery, mix well and microwave on **HIGH (100%) 3 MINUTES**.

2. Transfer roux to a 3-quart casserole. Add tomatoes and green chilies, tomato sauce, salt, pepper and garlic powder. Microwave on **HIGH (100%) 5 MINUTES**, stirring once.

3. Add shrimp, cover and microwave on **HIGH (100%) 10 MINUTES**, stirring once or twice. Let stand 10 minutes. Serve over steamed rice.

SHRIMP EGGPLANT PIE
gamberetti e melanzane infornati

Cooking Time: 21 minutes
Utensils: 1½-quart glass dish
2-quart glass dish
Servings: 4

1 pound shrimp, peeled
1 teaspoon Creole seasoning
1 chicken bouillon cube,
crushed

1. Place shrimp in a 1½-quart dish. Sprinkle with Creole seasoning, cover and microwave on **HIGH (100%) 5 MINUTES**. Stir one time. Drain and reserve 1/2 cup shrimp stock. Dissolve bouillon cube in stock and set aside.

1/4 cup margarine
1 small onion (2/3 cup),
chopped
1 stalk celery (1/3 cup),
chopped
1 green bell pepper (1/2 cup),
chopped
1 large (1½-lb.) eggplant
peeled, diced in 1/2-inch
cubes

2. Micromelt margarine in a 2-quart dish on **HIGH (100%) 1 MINUTE**. Add onion, celery and bell pepper. Sauté covered on **HIGH (100%) 3 MINUTES**. Add diced eggplant, cover and microwave on **HIGH (100%) 8 MINUTES**. Stir once. Drain.

1/2 cup shrimp stock
2 Tablespoons Vermouth
1/2 cup bread crumbs
1 teaspoon salt
Freshly ground pepper
1/2 cup Parmesan cheese,
grated

3. To the eggplant add shrimp, shrimp stock, Vermouth, bread crumbs, salt and pepper. Top with grated Parmesan cheese. Microwave on **HIGH (100%) 4 MINUTES**, rotate dish once.

61

JALAPEÑO SHRIMP

camarones jalapeño

Cooking Time: 20 minutes
Utensils: 2-quart glass casserole
4-cup glass measuring cup
Servings: 6

1½ pounds shrimp, peeled
Red and black pepper to
sprinkle
2 slices lemon
2 slices onion
1/2 stalk celery with leaves
1/4 teaspoon salt

1. Place shrimp in a 2-quart dish. Season with red and black pepper. Add lemon, onion and celery. Cover and microwave on **HIGH (100%) 8 MINUTES** or until shrimp turn light pink, stirring once. Drain and reserve stock for another recipe (can be frozen). Add salt to shrimp, cover and set aside.

4 Tablespoons margarine
1/2 cup celery, chopped
1/4 cup green onions,
chopped

2. Melt margarine on **HIGH (100%) 1 MINUTE** in a 4-cup measure. Add celery and onions. Sauté on **HIGH (100%) 3–4 MINUTES**.

4 Tablespoons flour
1/2 cup half and half cream
1 (6-oz.) roll jalapeño cheese,
cubed
3/4 teaspoon salt
Seasoned bread crumbs

3. Stir in flour and add cream slowly. Add cheese and salt. Microwave on **HIGH (100%) 2 MINUTES** or until cheese melts, stirring once. Pour cheese sauce over drained shrimp. Sprinkle with bread crumbs. Microwave on **HIGH (100%) 5 MINUTES** or until heated through.

SHRIMP LAVONNE

crevettes lavonne

Cooking Time: 15 minutes
Utensils: 2-quart glass casserole
4-cup glass measuring cup
7 x 11-inch glass baking dish
Servings: 6

2 pounds shrimp, peeled and cooked
1 cup rice, cooked
1 cup sharp Cheddar cheese, grated
1 (10-oz.) can mushroom soup, undiluted
1/2 teaspoon salt
1/4 teaspoon red pepper

1. Place shrimp in a 2-quart dish. Cover and microwave on **HIGH (100%) 5 MINUTES** or until shrimp turn light pink. Stir once. Drain. Stir in cooked rice, cheese, mushroom soup, salt and pepper.

1/4 cup margarine
1/2 cup green bell pepper, chopped
1/2 cup green onion tops, chopped
1/2 cup celery, chopped

2. In a 4-cup measure melt margarine on **HIGH (100%) 1 MINUTE**. Add bell pepper, onion tops and celery and sauté on **HIGH (100%) 4 MINUTES**. Add to shrimp mixture and put into a flat baking dish.

3 lemons

3. Cut lemons into 12 slices. Completely cover top of shrimp mixture with sliced lemons. Cover with wax paper and microwave on **HIGH (100%) 10 MINUTES**.

SHRIMP PONTCHARTRAIN
crevettes pontchartrain

Cooking Time: 16 minutes
Utensils: 1½-quart glass dish
            2-quart glass dish
Servings: 6–8

1½ pounds shrimp, peeled
1 teaspoon Creole seasoning
(or your favorite
seasoning)

1. Place shrimp in a 1½-quart dish. Sprinkle with Creole seasoning. Cover. Microwave on **HIGH (100%) 5 MINUTES**, stirring once. Drain, reserve 1/2 cup shrimp stock. Set shrimp aside covered.

1/2 cup margarine
1/2 bunch (1 cup) green
   onions, tops and bulbs
   chopped
6 fresh mushrooms, sliced

2. In a 2-quart dish melt margarine on **HIGH (100%) 1 MINUTE**. Add green onions and mushrooms, sauté on **HIGH (100%) 3 MINUTES**.

1/4 cup flour
1/2 cup shrimp stock
1/2 cup half and half cream
   (warmed on HIGH
   (100%) 30 SECONDS)
1/4 cup Vermouth
1 teaspoon salt
1/4 teaspoon white pepper
1/4 teaspoon cayenne pepper
Pastry shells for serving

3. Stir in flour. Slowly add stock, cream, Vermouth, salt, white pepper and cayenne pepper. Blend well. Drain shrimp again before adding to mixture. Microwave on **HIGH (100%) 7 MINUTES**, stirring 2 times. Place mixture in pastry shells or individual ramekins and serve with fresh asparagus, if desired.

64

SHRIMP WITH ARTICHOKES AND MUSHROOMS

gamberetti con carciofi e funghi

Cooking Time: 13 minutes
Utensil: 2-quart glass casserole
Servings: 4–6

1/4 cup margarine
1 pound shrimp, peeled
1 teaspoon seasoned salt

1. Micromelt margarine in a 2-quart casserole on **HIGH (100%) 1 MINUTE**. Stir in shrimp, cover and microwave on **HIGH (100%) 5 MINUTES**, stirring once, until shrimp are pink. Remove shrimp with a slotted spoon to another dish, sprinkle with seasoned salt and set aside covered.

6 Tablespoons flour
1 teaspoon onion salt
1½ cups half and half cream
or canned evaporated
milk, undiluted

2. Add flour and onion salt to margarine in the 2-quart dish. Add milk gradually, using a whisk until blended. Microwave on **HIGH (100%) 4 MINUTES**, stirring twice, until smooth and thick.

1/3 cup Vermouth or dry
white wine
1/2 teaspoon salt
1/4 teaspoon Tabasco
1 (6-oz.) jar marinated
artichoke hearts,
drained and quartered
1 (4-oz.) can mushrooms,
drained and sliced

3. Blend in Vermouth, salt and Tabasco. Add artichokes, mushrooms and cooked shrimp. Cover and microwave on **HIGH (100%) 2 to 3 MINUTES** until thoroughly heated. Serve on a bed of parsley buttered rice.

SHRIMP SOUFFLÉ

soufflé aux crevettes

Cooking Time: 15 minutes
Utensils: 2-quart glass casserole
3-quart glass casserole
Servings: 4–6

2 cups shrimp, peeled
Red and black pepper to
sprinkle
2 slices lemon
2 slices onion
1/2 stalk celery with leaves
1/4 teaspoon salt

1. Place shrimp in a 2-quart dish. Season with red and black pepper. Add lemon, onion and celery. Cover and microwave on **HIGH (100%) 5 MINUTES** or until shrimp turn light pink. Stir once. Drain and reserve stock for another recipe. Add salt to shrimp, cover and set aside.

4 slices bread, cut into 1/2-
inch squares
1/4 cup green onions,
chopped
2 cups mild Cheddar cheese,
grated
1 Tablespoon dry mustard

2. Cover bottom of a buttered 3-quart dish with bread squares then a layer of shrimp, onion and cheese, alternating until dish is filled ending with cheese on top. Sprinkle with mustard.

3 eggs, beaten
1 cup milk
1/2 teaspoon salt
1/4 teaspoon red pepper
Paprika to sprinkle

3. Beat eggs, add milk, salt and pepper. Pour over casserole and sprinkle with paprika. Microwave on **HIGH (100%) 10 MINUTES**.

SHRIMP VERACRUZ

camarones a la Veracruzana

Cooking Time: 21 minutes
Utensils: 2-quart glass casserole
2-quart glass dish
Servings: 6 to 8

SAUCE:

2 Tablespoons margarine
2 large onions, sliced thinly
in rings
2 large green bell pepper,
seeded and sliced in
long strips

2 cups fresh tomatoes,
peeled, seeded and
juiced, cut in large
pieces
1 (4-oz.) can whole green
chilies, seeded and
chopped
2 teaspoons salt
1/4 teaspoon red pepper

SHRIMP:

1 Tablespoon margarine
1 Tablespoon vegetable oil
6 cloves garlic, minced
3 pounds large shrimp,
peeled and butterflied
(split slightly down
back)
1/4 cup white wine
1 teaspoon lemon juice
1 teaspoon salt
2 teaspoons Creole
seasoning (or your
favorite seasoning)

1. Micromelt margarine in a 2-quart casserole. Mix in onions and bell pepper, cover with plastic wrap and microwave on **HIGH (100%) 5 MINUTES** until softened.

2. Add tomatoes, green chilies, salt and pepper. Cover with a paper towel and microwave on **HIGH (100%) 4 MINUTES**, stirring, once. Cover and set aside.

3. Micromelt margarine and oil in a 2-quart dish on **HIGH (100%) 1 MINUTE**. Add garlic and sauté on **HIGH (100%) 2 MINUTES**. Stir in shrimp, wine and lemon juice. Cover and microwave on **HIGH (100%) 9 MINUTES**. Stir and rearrange shrimp 3 times so all will be pink. After cooking, add salt and Creole seasoning. Stir shrimp into sauce and serve over Arroz Verde (Green Rice) Page 130. Shrimp Veracruz may be prepared earlier. Before serving, microwave on **HIGH (100%) 3 MINUTES**.

AVOCADO ST. JACQUES

avocat st. jacques

Cooking Time: 22 minutes
Utensils: 8-inch square glass dish
2-quart glass bowl
8-cup glass measuring cup
Servings: 6

2 pounds scallops, washed

1. Cut scallops in large bite-size pieces. Place in an 8-inch square dish. Cover with plastic wrap and poach on **HIGH (100%) 8–10 MINUTES**, stirring once to rearrange. Drain and measure 3/4 cup liquid. Cover scallops to keep warm.

3/4 cup dry white wine
3/4 cup scallop liquid
1/4 cup onion, minced
2 teaspoons parsley, minced
1/2 teaspoon salt
1/4 teaspoon thyme
1/2 bay leaf
1/2 pound fresh mushrooms, sliced

2. In a 2-quart bowl combine wine, scallop liquid, onion, parsley, salt, thyme and bay leaf. Microwave on **HIGH (100%) 3 MINUTES**. Stir in mushrooms and poached scallops. Cover and microwave on **HIGH (100%) 3 MINUTES**. To test a scallop for doneness let stand 1 minute. When cut, inside texture should be flaky. Strain and reserve 1½ cups stock for sauce. Set scallops aside covered.

SAUCE:

1/4 cup margarine
1/4 cup flour
1½ cups stock from scallops
1/4 cup whipping cream
2/3 cup Hollandaise Sauce (see page 56, or use 1 (6-oz.) can prepared Hollandaise Sauce)
1/4 teaspoon salt
1/8 teaspoon white pepper
3 ripe avocados, halved

3. Micromelt margarine in an 8-cup measure. Add flour and gradually stir in stock. Microwave on **HIGH (100%) 5–6 MINUTES** until thickened, stirring at 1 minute intervals after the first 2 minutes. Stir in cream, Hollandaise Sauce, salt and pepper. Add scallops and mushrooms. Fill peeled avocado halves with scallop mixture. Serve immediately.

SEAFOOD LASAGNA

lasagne con frutti di mare

Cooking Time: 29 minutes
Utensils: 1½-quart glass dish
        7 x 11-inch glass baking dish
        4-cup glass measuring cup
        8-cup glass measuring cup
Servings: 12

1½ pounds shrimp, peeled
Cayenne pepper for
   sprinkling
1 slice onion
1 slice lemon

1. Place shrimp sprinkled with pepper, onion and lemon in a 1½-quart dish. Cover. Microwave on **HIGH (100%) 5–7 MINUTES** until all shrimp are pink. Stir once. Drain and set aside.

8 lasagne noodles

2. Cook lasagna noodles according to package directions, *al dente* (approximately 10 minutes). Drain. Arrange 4 noodles on bottom of greased 7 x 11-inch baking dish.

2 Tablespoons margarine
1 cup onion, chopped
1 (8-oz.) package cream
   cheese, softened
1½ cups cream style cottage
   cheese or ricotta
1 egg, beaten
2 teaspoons dried basil
1 teaspoon salt
1/2 teaspoon Creole
   seasoning
1/2 teaspoon red pepper

3. Micromelt margarine in a 4-cup measure. Add onion and sauté on **HIGH (100%) 2 MINUTES** until tender; blend in cream cheese. Stir in cottage cheese or ricotta, egg, basil, salt, Creole seasoning and pepper. Spread half of cheese mixture on the 4 noodles.

2 (10 ¾-oz.) cans cream of
   mushroom soup,
   undiluted
1/3 cup milk
1/3 cup dry white wine
1 pound white lump crab
   meat
1 (12-oz.) package Mozzarella
   cheese, 8 slices
1/4 cup Parmesan cheese,
   grated

4. In an 8-cup measure combine soup, milk and wine. Stir in cooked shrimp and crab. Spread on half this mixture. Lay 4 slices of Mozzarella cheese on top. Repeat layers starting with remaining noodles. Sprinkle Parmesan cheese on top. Microwave on **HIGH (100%) 10 MINUTES** or until heated through. Rotate dish 2 times. Top with remaining Mozzarella slices after cooking. Freezes well.

Poultry

Game

Poultry:
aves de corral   *Spanish*
pollame   *Italian*
volailles   *French*

Now, microwaving the turkey, chicken or game frees the holiday cook to have as much fun as the holiday guests.

ARTICHOKE CHICKEN

pollo con alcachofa

With sour cream sauce

Cooking Time: 10 minutes
Utensils: 9-inch browning dish with cover
Servings: 4–6

1 cup sour cream
2 Tablespoons fresh parsley,
    chopped
1/2 teaspoon salt
1 Tablespoon fresh lemon
    juice

1/4 cup margarine, melted
4 whole chicken breasts (2
    pounds) boned, cut in
    bite-size pieces
2 medium onions, thinly
    sliced

1 teaspoon instant chicken
    bouillon
1 (4-oz.) can sliced
    mushrooms, drained;
    reserve 1/4 cup liquid
2 (8½-oz.) cans artichoke
    hearts, drained and
    sliced in half
1/2 teaspoon thyme
1/2 teaspoon basil
1/2 teaspoon salt
1/8 teaspoon pepper

1. Mix sour cream, parsley, salt and lemon juice in a small serving bowl. Refrigerate several hours to enhance flavor of the sauce.*

2. Preheat empty browning dish on **HIGH (100%) 4 MINUTES**. Then add margarine and quickly sear chicken pieces. Add onions, cover and microwave on **HIGH (100%) 3 MINUTES**.

3. Dissolve bouillon in mushroom liquid and stir into chicken. Add mushrooms, sliced artichoke hearts, thyme, basil, salt and pepper. Stir to mix well. Cover and microwave on **HIGH (100%) 3 MINUTES** until tender. Do not overcook. Let stand covered 5 minutes. Serve sour cream sauce* over each portion.

BAKED CHICKEN BREASTS

blanc de volaille au four

Cooking Time: 11 minutes
Utensils: 2 quart dish
          8-inch square glass dish
          1-cup glass measuring cup
Servings: 4–6

**6 chicken breast halves,
    skinned and boned**
1 cup dairy sour cream
2 Tablespoons lemon juice
**2 teaspoons Worcestershire
    sauce**
1/2 teaspoon celery salt
1 teaspoon paprika
1/4 teaspoon garlic powder
1½ teaspoons salt
1/4 teaspoon red pepper

**1 cup seasoned bread
    crumbs**
1/4 cup margarine

1. Rinse and dry 6 chicken breast halves with paper towels. In a 2-quart dish combine sour cream, lemon juice, Worcestershire sauce, celery salt, paprika, garlic powder, salt and pepper. Add chicken to sour cream mixture, coating each piece well. Let stand, covered, in refrigerator overnight or at least eight hours.

2. Carefully remove coated chicken from sour cream mixture. Roll in crumbs, coating evenly. Arrange single layer in an 8-inch square shallow baking dish. Micromelt margarine in a 1-cup measure on **HIGH (100%) 1 MINUTE** and drizzle over chicken. Microwave on **HIGH (100%) 10 MINUTES** or until chicken is tender.

CHICKEN BREASTS WITH TARRAGON SAUCE
petti di pollo con salsa al 'tarragon'

Cooking Time: 11 minutes
Utensils: 2-quart glass dish
  4-cup glass measuring cup
Servings: 4–6

3/4 cup chicken stock or broth
3/4 cup dry white wine
4 whole chicken breasts, split, skinned, boned (about 1½ pounds)

1. Bring stock and wine to a boil in a 2-quart dish on **HIGH (100%) 4 MINUTES**. Cut chicken breasts in half and add to liquid. Cover and microwave on **HIGH (100%) 2 MINUTES**. Do not overcook. Transfer chicken to a covered dish. Reserve stock for sauce.

3 egg yolks
2 Tablespoons cornstarch
1 cup whipping cream
1 Tablespoon tarragon*
2 teaspoons salt
1/4 teaspoon celery salt
1/4 teaspoon white pepper
1 (17-oz.) can green peas, Petit Pois, drained
Snipped parsley to sprinkle
Cooked buttered noodles for 4–6

2. Whisk egg yolks and cornstarch in a 4-cup measure. Add cream and 1/4 cup of hot cooking stock. Whisk egg mixture into remaining stock. Add tarragon, salt, celery salt and white pepper. Microwave sauce on **HIGH (100%) 5 MINUTES**, until thickened, stirring every minute. Fold in peas and chicken pieces. Sprinkle with parsley and serve with buttered noodles.

MICRO MEMO:

The oil and fragrance of * tarragon will be released by rubbing the dried leaves in the palm of your hand as it is added to the sauce.

CHICKEN CACCIATORE

pollo al cacciatore

Cooking Time: 42 minutes
Utensils: 10 x 10-inch ceramic baking dish
        3-quart glass or ceramic casserole
Servings: 6

1 (3-lb.) chicken, skinned and cut in pieces
Micro-Shake to sprinkle

1. Season chicken pieces with Micro-Shake or an all-purpose seasoning. Place in a 10 x 10-inch baking dish. Cover and microwave on **HIGH (100%) 18 MINUTES** until partially done. Set aside covered.

3/4 cup green bell pepper, chopped
2 cups onion, chopped
3 cloves garlic, crushed
2 Tablespoons olive oil

2. Sauté bell pepper, onion, garlic and oil in a 3-quart casserole on **HIGH (100%) 5–6 MINUTES**.

4 large tomatoes, peeled and chopped
1/2 teaspoon basil
1/2 teaspoon oregano
1/2 teaspoon thyme
1 teaspoon salt
1/4 teaspoon pepper
5 large fresh mushrooms, sliced
Cooked noodles for 6

3. Add tomatoes, basil, oregano, thyme, salt and pepper to onion mixture. Microwave on **HIGH (100%) 10 MINUTES**. Add mushrooms and cooked chicken (bone if desired). Cover and microwave on **HIGH (100%) 7–8 MINUTES** or until chicken is tender. Serve over noodles.

CHICKEN CHILAQUILES

pollo chilaquiles
Pronounced POH-yoh chee-lah-KEE-lehs

Tortillas with chicken and chili sauce

Cooking Time: Chicken 30 minutes
Casserole 11 minutes
Utensils: 4-cup glass measuring cup
7 x 11-inch glass baking dish
Servings: 8

1 (3-lb.) chicken, cut in pieces

1. Follow directions on page 79 for "Cooked Chicken". Bone and dice chicken, reserving stock.

SAUCE:

1 (10-oz.) can Ro-tel tomatoes and green chilies, chopped with liquid
1/2 teaspoon salt
1/2 cup chicken stock
1 (10¾-oz.) can cream of chicken soup, undiluted
1 (10¾-oz.) can cream of mushroom soup, undiluted

2. Combine tomatoes and green chilies, salt, chicken stock, chicken soup and mushroom soup in a 4-cup measure. Blend well.

TO ASSEMBLE:

12 corn tortillas, broken into quarters
2 cups cooked chicken
2 cups onion, finely chopped
3 cups sharp Cheddar cheese, grated (about 12 ounces)

3. In a greased 7 x 11-inch baking dish place one-third each of tortillas, diced chicken, sauce, chopped onions, and grated cheese. Repeat in this order, twice more, ending with cheese on top. Microwave on **HIGH (100%) 11 MIN-UTES**, rotating dish after half the cooking time. Let stand 5 minutes before serving.

CHICKEN ENCHILADAS
enchiladas de pollo

Cooking Time: Chicken 25 minutes
                Enchiladas 19 minutes
Utensils: 2-quart round glass dish
          4-cup measuring cup
          7 x 11-inch glass baking dish
Servings: 6

1 (3-lb.) chicken, cut in pieces

1. Microwave chicken according to directions for "Cooked Chicken" on page 79. Bone and dice chicken for filling.

1½ cups whipping cream
4 chicken bouillon cubes

FILLING:

2. In a 2-quart round dish heat cream and chicken bouillon cubes on **HIGH (100%) 2–3 MINUTES**, stirring once to help dissolve cubes. Set aside.

2 Tablespoons vegetable oil
1 cup onion, chopped
1 clove garlic, crushed
2 (4¾-oz.) cans tomato purée
4 whole canned green chilies, seeded and chopped
1 teaspoon salt
2 cups cooked chicken, diced

3. Place oil, onion, and garlic in a 4-cup measure. Sauté on **HIGH (100%) 3 MINUTES**. Add tomato, chilies, salt and diced chicken. Microwave on **HIGH (100%) 4 MINUTES**.

TO ASSEMBLE:

12 flour or corn tortillas
1/2 pound Monterey Jack or Swiss cheese, grated

4. Wrap tortillas in a wet dish towel and microwave on **HIGH (100%) 45 SECONDS**. Dip each tortilla in bouillon cream mixture. Fill generously with chicken mixture and roll up, placing seam side down in a 7 x 11-inch baking dish. Pour remaining cream mixture over tortillas. Top with grated cheese. Microwave on **HIGH (100%) 8 MINUTES**.

CHICKEN TAMALE PIE

pastel de pollo y tamales

Cooking Time: Chicken 20 minutes
Pie 15 minutes
Utensils: 2-quart glass casserole
4-cup glass measuring cup
7 x 11-inch glass baking dish
Servings: 8–9

6 chicken thighs (about 1¾ pounds)
All-purpose seasoning
2 slices onion
1 stalk celery with leaves
2½ cups water
1 teaspoon salt dissolved in water
1/2 teaspoon red pepper

SAUCE:

1 teaspoon vegetable oil
1 cup onion, chopped
2 cloves garlic, minced
1 (4¾-oz.) can tomato purée
1 cup chicken stock
1/8 teaspoon marjoram
1/8 teaspoon thyme
1 teaspoon chili powder
1 bay leaf
1 (17-oz.) can whole kernel corn, drained
1/2 cup ripe olives, sliced
Shredded cooked chicken

18 tamales, shucked and cut lengthwise through center
1 pound mild Cheddar cheese, grated

1. Sprinkle chicken with an all-purpose seasoning. Place chicken, onion, celery, salted water and pepper in a 2-quart casserole. Cover. Microwave on **HIGH (100%) 18 to 20 MINUTES**. Shred chicken with a fork. Reserve chicken and 1 cup of stock for sauce.

2. Sauté oil, onion and garlic in a 4-cup measure on **HIGH (100%) 3–4 MINUTES**, until limp. Add tomato purée, chicken stock, marjoram, thyme, chili powder and bay leaf. Bring to a boil on **HIGH (100%) 4 MINUTES**, stirring one time. Add corn, ripe olives and shredded chicken.

3. Layer half the tamales, cut-side up, in a greased 7 x 11-inch baking dish. Pour half the sauce over tamales and sprinkle on half the cheese. Repeat layers ending with cheese on top. Microwave on **HIGH (100%) 7 MINUTES** until heated through. Rotate dish once.

"COOKED CHICKEN"

poulet poche

Cooking Time: 25 minutes
Utensil: 3-quart casserole
Yields: 2 cups boned chicken
       and 3 cups stock

Prepare chicken, reserve stock, bone chicken and use in any recipe calling for "cooked chicken." Keep in refrigerator or freezer until ready to use.

2½ to 3 pound chicken
1/2 onion, sliced
1 stalk cut celery and leaves
1/4 cup white wine
3 cups hot water
1 teaspoon salt
1/2 teaspoon cayenne pepper

Place chicken, onion, celery, wine, water and seasonings in a 3-quart casserole. Cover. Microwave on **HIGH (100%) 25 MINUTES**.

CHICKEN OF THE RITZ

poulet au ritz

Cooking Time: 21 minutes
Utensils: Glass pie plate
         10-inch square glass dish
Servings: 4

2½ pounds chicken breasts
    and thighs, skinned
Red pepper to sprinkle

1. Season chicken pieces with red pepper or your favorite seasoning mixture. (Add salt after cooking.)

1/2 cup margarine
2 cloves garlic, pressed
2 Tablespoons chopped
    parsley

2. Melt margarine in a glass pie plate on **HIGH (100%) 1 MINUTE**. Add garlic and parsley.

2 cups coarsely crushed Ritz
    crackers

3. Roll chicken pieces in margarine mixture, then coat with Ritz cracker crumbs. Place in a 10-inch square glass dish. Cover with paper towel. Microwave on **HIGH (100%) 20 MINUTES** until tender and done.

CREAMED CHICKEN CASSEROLE

volaille béchamel

Cooking Time: 12 minutes
Utensils: 8 x 8-inch glass baking dish
5 x 9-inch glass or ceramic loaf dish or 4 individual ceramic gratin dishes
Servings: 4

1 pound fresh broccoli or 1 (10-oz.) carton frozen broccoli spears
2 Tablespoons water
1/2 teaspoon salt, to sprinkle after cooking

1. Rinse broccoli, cut into spears and trim tough stems. Place in an 8 x 8-inch baking dish with stems toward outer edge of dish. Add 2 tablespoons water, cover with plastic wrap and steam on **HIGH (100%) 6 MINUTES** until tender. Sprinkle salt on after cooking. *Alternate*: If using frozen broccoli spears, remove outer waxed wrapper, place carton in dish and microwave on **HIGH (100%) 6 MINUTES**. Drain. Add salt after cooking. Cover and set aside.

1 (10¾-oz.) can cream of mushroom soup, undiluted
1 (10¾-oz.) can cream of chicken soup, undiluted
2 (5-oz.) cans Swanson chicken
1/4 teaspoon white pepper

2. Mix mushroom soup, chicken soup, chicken and pepper in a 5 x 9-inch serving dish. Microwave on **HIGH (100%) 4 MINUTES**, stirring 1 time.

1 cup Cheddar cheese, grated

3. Add steamed broccoli spears, arranging so stems are immersed in creamed chicken sauce. Top with cheese, cover and microwave on **HIGH (100%) 2 MINUTES** until heated through. If using individual gratin dishes, heat 2 at a time on **HIGH (100%) 1 MINUTE**.

ENCHILADAS CAMPECHE

Cooking Time: Chicken 25 minutes
Enchiladas 22 minutes
Utensils: 8-cup glass measuring cup
2-quart glass dish
7 x 11-inch glass baking dish
Servings: 6

1 (3–3½ lb.) chicken, cut in pieces

1. Microwave chicken according to directions for "Cooked Chicken" on page 79. Reserve and freeze stock for another recipe.

CHILI SAUCE:

2 cups onion, finely chopped
1 clove garlic, minced
1 Tablespoon vegetable oil
1½ cups canned green chilies, rinsed, seeded, chopped
5 ripe tomatoes, peeled and chopped
1/8 teaspoon oregano
2 teaspoons salt
1/4 teaspoon pepper
2 Tablespoons flour

2. In an 8-cup measure sauté onion, garlic and oil on **HIGH (100%) 3 MINUTES**. Add chilies, tomatoes, oregano, salt and pepper. Microwave on **HIGH (100%) 7 MINUTES**, stirring once. In a small bowl mix flour with a small amount of the hot tomato mixture to make a paste. Stir back into tomato mixture. Microwave on **HIGH (100%) 4 MINUTES**, stirring once. Set aside while preparing the enchiladas.

CHICKEN ENCHILADAS:

4 cups cooked chicken, diced
1/2 pound Cheddar cheese, grated
1 pint dairy sour cream
12 corn tortillas

3. In a 2-quart dish mix chicken, cheese and sour cream together. Soften the tortillas by dipping each tortilla in warm liquid from the prepared chili sauce. Fill each tortilla with chicken mixture and roll, placing seam side down in a greased 7 x 11-inch baking dish. Pour chili sauce over enchiladas. Microwave on **HIGH (100%) 8 MINUTES**, turning dish one time.

ENCHILADAS MONTEREY

Cooking Time: Chicken 25 minutes
Enchiladas 15 minutes
Utensils: 4-cup glass measuring cup
7 x 11-inch glass baking dish
Servings: 6

1 (3-lb.) chicken, cut in pieces

1. Microwave chicken according to directions for "Cooked Chicken" on page 79. Bone and chop chicken for filling. Reserve stock.

SAUCE:

1/2 cup vegetable oil
1/2 cup flour
1⅓ cup onions, chopped
2 whole canned green chilies, seeded and chopped
2 cups chicken stock
1½ teaspoon salt
1/8 teaspoon white pepper
1/8 teaspoon basil
1/2 cup heavy cream

2. Completely mix oil and flour together in a 4-cup measure until smooth. Microwave on **HIGH (100%) 5 MINUTES** to reach a "blonde" or pale roux. Stir in onions and chilies and microwave on **HIGH (100%) 3 MINUTES**. Add chicken stock, salt, white pepper, basil and cream.

FILLING:

4 ounces cream cheese
4 ounces dairy sour cream
3 whole canned jalapeño peppers, seeded and chopped
2½–3 cups cooked chicken, chopped
1 teaspoon salt
1/8 teaspoon white pepper

3. In a mixing bowl blend cream cheese and sour cream. Stir in peppers, chopped chicken, salt and pepper.

12 soft corn tortillas
2 cups Monterey Jack cheese, grated
1/2 cup dairy sour cream

4. Dip tortillas into warm chicken stock. Spoon generous portions of filling onto each tortilla along with a small amount of sauce. Roll and place seam side down in a greased 7 x 11-inch baking dish. Pour remaining sauce over the enchiladas and spoon sour cream over the top. Sprinkle grated cheese on top and microwave on **HIGH (100%) 7 MINUTES**. Turn dish once.

ENCHILADAS SALTILLO

Pronounced in-chee-LAH-thah sal-t-o

Cooking Time: Chicken 25 minutes
Enchiladas 12 minutes
Utensils: 4-cup glass measuring cup
7 x 11-inch glass baking dish
Servings: 6

1 (2½–3 lb.) chicken, cut in pieces

1. Microwave chicken according to directions for "Cooked Chicken" on page 79. Set aside 1 cup of stock to soften tortillas. Reserve remaining stock for another recipe. Bone and chop chicken for filling.

SAUCE:

1 (16-oz.) can tomatoes, drained
1 (4-oz.) can whole green chilies, drained and seeded
1/2 teaspoon ground coriander
1 teaspoon salt
1 cup dairy sour cream

2. Place tomatoes, chilies, coriander and salt in blender. Process until smooth. Add sour cream to blend. Set aside.

FILLING:

1 teaspoon margarine
1/4 cup onion, finely chopped
1 (3-oz.) package cream cheese, softened
2 cups cooked chicken, finely chopped

3. Micromelt margarine in a 4-cup measure. Stir in onions and microwave on **HIGH (100%) 2 MINUTES**. Add cream cheese and blend well. Add cooked chicken and stir to mix.

12 flour tortillas
2 cups Monterey Jack cheese, grated

4. Place equal amounts of chicken mixture in each tortilla. Roll and place seam side down in a 7 x 11-inch baking dish. Pour tomato and chili sauce over enchiladas. Cover and microwave on **HIGH (100%) 7 MINUTES**. Rotate dish one time. Sprinkle on cheese and microwave uncovered on **HIGH (100%) 3 MINUTES**.

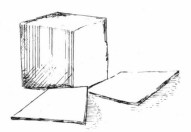

POULET ALEXANDRA

Cooking Time: 12 minutes 30 seconds
Utensils: 4-cup glass measuring cup
         10-inch shallow ceramic dish
Servings: 4–6

1/4 pound mushrooms
1/4 cup fresh parsley
1/4 cup green onions
1 Tablespoon margarine
3/4 cup seasoned bread
    crumbs
2 Tablespoons white wine

1. To prepare stuffing, chop mushrooms, parsley and green onions. Micromelt margarine in a 4-cup measure on **HIGH (100%) 30 SECONDS**. Add mushrooms, parsley and onions and sauté on **HIGH (100%) 2 MINUTES**. Stir in bread crumbs and wine.

6 chicken breast halves,
    skinned and boned

2. Place 2 tablespoons stuffing on each breast. Roll and secure with a wooden pick. Lightly grease a shallow 10-inch dish. Place stuffed breasts in dish, cover and microwave on **HIGH (100%) 10 MINUTES**. Rearrange stuffed breasts in dish after half the cooking time.

POULET KIEV

From Chinon, France

Cooking Time: 19 minutes 30 seconds
Utensils: 9-inch browning dish with lid
2-cup glass measuring cup
Servings: 4–6

1/2 cup butter
2 Tablespoons parsley, minced
2 Tablespoons tarragon leaves, crushed
2 Tablespoons chives, minced
1 clove garlic, minced

8 chicken breast halves, about 1¾ pounds, skinned and boned (keep bones and make stock with them!)
White pepper and an all-purpose seasoning to sprinkle
Flour for coating
1 egg, beaten
1/2 cup (or more) bread crumbs
2 Tablespoons butter

SAUCE:

1 Tablespoon butter
2 Tablespoons flour
1 teaspoon Worcestershire sauce
1/4 teaspoon ground turmeric
1 Tablespoon dry mustard
1/2 teaspoon salt
1/4 teaspoon white pepper
1 cup chicken stock

1. Blend butter, parsley, tarragon, chives and garlic with a fork. Roll mixture into 8 balls and place in the freezer to harden. This can be prepared ahead.

2. Flatten chicken breasts with a mallet or edge of a saucer and season both sides with pepper and an all-purpose seasoning (not salt). Place a frozen butter ball on each breast. Fold chicken over, envelope shape, to enclose ball. Tie bundles with string or secure with wooden picks for sautéing. Preheat empty browning dish on **HIGH (100%) 4 MINUTES**. Dip chicken bundles into flour to coat, then egg and roll in bread crumbs. Melt butter in browning dish and quickly brown the 8 chicken bundles turning each with a wooden spoon. Cover dish and microwave on **HIGH (100%) 5 MINUTES**. Discard liquid, cover chicken and set aside while preparing sauce.

3. Micromelt butter in a 2-cup measure on **HIGH (100%) 30 SECONDS**. Stir in flour, add Worcestershire, turmeric, dry mustard, salt and pepper. Slowly add chicken stock and blend well. Microwave on **HIGH (100%) 5 MINUTES** until thickened, stirring at 2 minute intervals. Pour sauce over chicken, cover and microwave on **HIGH (100%) 5 MINUTES**. Serve over noodles or rice.

85

ROAST CHICKEN I

Cooking Time: 30 minutes
Utensils: 2 or 3-quart glass baking dish
Servings: 6

1 (3-lb.) whole fryer
Micro-Shake
Creole seasoning (or your
 favorite seasoning)
Kitchen Bouquet

1. Rinse and season chicken with Micro-Shake and Creole seasoning inside and out. Pour Kitchen Bouquet into hand and rub entire fryer.

1 onion, quartered
1/2 green bell pepper, sliced
1 stalk celery with leaves, cut
 in 2 or 3 pieces

2. Stuff chicken with onion, bell pepper and celery. Place chicken, breast side down, in baking dish. Tent with wax paper. Microwave on **HIGH (100%) 15 MINUTES**. Rotate dish once. Turn chicken breast up, tent with wax paper and finish cooking on **HIGH (100%) 15 MINUTES**. Rotate dish once.

ROAST CHICKEN II

Cooking Time: 25 minutes
Utensil: 2-quart round casserole
Servings: 6

1 (3-lb.) whole chicken
Garlic and onion powder to
 sprinkle

1. Sprinkle inside of chicken with garlic and onion powder. Stuff cavities with dressing by following recipe for Cornbread Dressing on page 129. Use wooden picks to close cavities.

1 teaspoon garlic powder
1 teaspoon onion powder
2 Tablespoons Kitchen
 Bouquet
1/4 cup white wine

2. Make a mixture of garlic and onion powder, Kitchen Bouquet and wine. Brush mixture over chicken. Place stuffed chicken, breast down, in a 2-quart round casserole. Cover with a tent of wax paper. Microwave on **HIGH (100%) 10 MINUTES**. Turn chicken over, cover and microwave on **HIGH (100%) 15 MINUTES**. Baste chicken 3 times.

SPAGHETTI DEVONSHIRE

Cooking Time: Spaghetti Sauce 38 minutes
Utensils: 3-quart glass or ceramic casserole
          2-quart glass casserole
Servings: 8

1 (8-oz.) package thin spaghetti (broken)

1. Cook spaghetti according to package directions.

1 (2½-lb.) chicken, cut in pieces
2 cups water
1/2 onion, sliced
1 stalk celery, cut in 3 pieces
1 teaspoon salt
1/2 teaspoon red pepper

2. Place chicken, water, onion, celery, salt and pepper in a 3-quart casserole. Cover and microwave on **HIGH (100%) 25 MINUTES**. Reserve and freeze stock for another recipe. Dice chicken and set aside.

3 Tablespoons butter
1/2 cup onion, chopped
1/2 cup green bell pepper, chopped
1 (16-oz.) can tomatoes with liquid, chopped
1 teaspoon salt
1/4 teaspoon pepper

3. Micromelt butter in a 2-quart casserole on **HIGH (100%) 1 MINUTE**. Add onion and bell pepper. Microwave on **HIGH (100%) 3 MINUTES**. Stir in tomatoes, salt and pepper. Cover and microwave on **HIGH (100%) 3 MINUTES**.

2 cups cooked chicken, diced
1 cup cooked ham, diced
1/2 pound Velveeta cheese, cubed
1/2 cup Velveeta cheese, grated

4. Add cooked spaghetti, diced chicken, ham and cubed cheese. Cover and microwave on **HIGH (100%) 6 MINUTES**. Sprinkle grated cheese on top and let sit covered for a few minutes before serving.

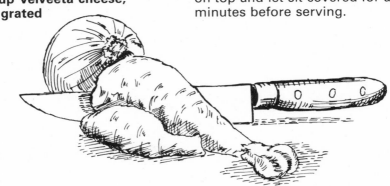

TURKEY À LA KING

Cooking Time: 11 minutes
Utensil: 2-quart glass dish
Servings: 6–8

1/2 cup margarine
1 large bunch green onions, tops
    and bulbs chopped
1 (8-oz.) can sliced mushrooms
1/2 cup parsley, chopped

4 Tablespoons flour
1 (13-oz.) can evaporated milk
1 cup Monterey Jack cheese or
    Mozzarella, grated
1 teaspoon salt
1/2 teaspoon cayenne pepper
1 Tablespoon Worcestershire
    sauce
2 Tablespoons pimiento,
    chopped
4 cups cooked turkey, cubed

1. Melt margarine in a 2-quart glass dish on **HIGH (100%) 1 MINUTE**. Add onions, mushrooms, and parsley and sauté on **HIGH (100%) 4 MINUTES**.

2. Stir in flour and add milk. Microwave on **HIGH (100%) 4 MINUTES** or until mixture is thick. Stir in cheese until melted. Add salt, pepper, Worcestershire, pimiento and turkey. Microwave on **HIGH (100%) 3 MINUTES** until warmed throughout. Serve on toasted English muffins or toast points.

TURKEY ENCHILADAS

Cooking Time: 4 minutes 45 seconds
Utensil: 7 x 11-inch glass baking dish
Servings: 6

1½ cups cooked turkey, coarsely
    chopped
1/2 cup shallots white bulb,
    chopped
2½ cups Cheddar cheese, grated
2 jalapeño peppers, fresh or
    canned, seeded and
    chopped
12 soft corn tortillas
1½ cups hot turkey or chicken
    stock

1. Wrap tortillas in a damp dish cloth. Microwave on **HIGH (100%) 45 SECONDS**. Dip tortillas in hot stock. Place small amount of chopped turkey, onion, cheese, jalapeño peppers and 1 tablespoon turkey stock on tortilla. Roll and place seam side down in a 7 x 11-inch glass baking dish.

2. Sprinkle any remaining cheese, onion, and peppers over top of enchiladas and add enough stock to keep enchiladas moist. Cover loosely with plastic wrap. Microwave on **HIGH (100%) 4 MINUTES** until cheese is melted and enchiladas are heated through. Serve with picante sauce or Mexican Dip on page 24.

HOW TO ROAST TURKEY

Defrost Time: Low (30%) 6–7 minutes per pound OR
Medium (50%) 4–5 minutes per pound
Cooking Time: High (100%) 5–6 minutes per pound
Utensils: Brown-In-Bag cooking bag (turkey size)
Large glass baking dish

1. SELECTING AND DEFROSTING TURKEY

   Select a 12 to 15-pound turkey with a round "shape", that is not too wide in the hips nor too high in the breast because it will be easier to turn turkey over in the microwave oven. Defrost turkey completely according to wrapper directions or using the microwave. Remove all metal clips and wrapper. Place in a Brown-In-Bag breast side down. Loosely close end of bag with a rubber band. Defrost on **MEDIUM (50%) 4–5 MINUTES PER POUND** or on **LOW (30%) 6–7 MINUTES PER POUND**. Turn turkey over 2 or 3 times to aid defrosting. Small strips of foil may be placed on back and breast bone to prevent dehydration. Before using foil, check your microwave manual on foil usage. Place turkey in cool water 20 to 30 minutes to remove giblets. Rinse and dry turkey.

2. SEASONING AND PREPARING FOR COOKING

   Season cavity with salt, red and black pepper, sage and celery salt. Your favorite dressing may be spooned into turkey cavity and the skin closed with a wooden pick.

   Tie legs and wings close to body with string. Rub exterior of turkey with vegetable oil and a liquid browning sauce such as Kitchen Bouquet or Bovril. Sprinkle paprika, Micro-Shake and any other seasoning, except salt, over entire turkey. Pierce skin with a fork to prevent splitting. Place turkey breast side down in Brown-In-Bag on a large glass plate or baking dish. Small strips of foil may be placed on the breast bone, legs and wing tips to shield these areas from overcooking. Close end of bag with a rubber band or a strip of plastic, leaving an opening at end of bag the size of a quarter.

3. COOKING TIME AND TEMPERATURE

   Weigh turkey and estimate total cooking time. Microwave on **HIGH (100%) 5–6 MINUTES PER POUND** or until temperature reaches 175 degrees in breast meat while cooking, and 185 degrees after standing 10 minutes. A strip of foil may be used to shield back and breast bone during the first 3/4 cooking time. Be sure to check your microwave manual on foil usage.

4. ROTATING AND TURNING TURKEY

   Rotate turkey 1/2 turn at 1/4 the cooking time. Turn turkey breast side up at 1/2 the cooking time. Rotate turkey 1/2 turn again at 3/4 the cooking time. A microwave thermometer could be inserted at this time. Baste off accumulated juices when turning to use later for gravy, gumbo and soup.

GAME

DAIGRE'S QUAIL SUPREME

caille suprême daigre

Cooking Time: 35 minutes
Utensils: 5-quart ceramic casserole
Servings: 6

12 quail or 4–5 whole chicken breasts, split in half
Pepper, paprika and garlic powder for sprinkling

2 packages dry onion soup mix
1 cup onion, chopped
2 slices bacon, uncooked and cut in pieces
1 (10-oz.) can cream of mushroom soup, undiluted
1 (4-oz.) can mushrooms, stems and pieces
2 Tablespoons parsley, chopped
1 teaspoon Kitchen Bouquet
1 chicken bouillon cube dissolved in 3/4 cup hot water
2 Tablespoons white wine

1. Sprinkle each quail or chicken breast with pepper, paprika and garlic powder. Place half the quail or chicken in a 4 or 5-quart casserole dish.

2. Layer 1 package dry onion soup, 1/2 cup onion, 1 slice of bacon pieces, 1/2 can cream of mushroom soup, 1/2 can mushrooms, 1 Tablespoon parsley and 1/2 teaspoon Kitchen Bouquet. Place remaining quail on top and layer ingredients in same order. Combine bouillon and wine. Pour over top. Cover and microwave on **HIGH (100%) 35 MINUTES** until quail are tender. Stir and rearrange quail at 15-minute intervals. Serve over rice or egg noodles. This dish may be prepared early. Let stand covered and reheat for 5 minutes on **HIGH (100%)**.

QUAIL CHEZ CUISINE

caille chez cuisine

Stuffed with hot sausage

Cooking Time: 17 minutes
Utensils: 6-pound size Brown-In-Bag
            9-inch round glass baking dish
Servings: 6

6 quail
Micro-Shake for sprinkling or
    an all-purpose
    seasoning

1. Rinse quail and dry with paper towels. Season with Micro-Shake or an all-purpose seasoning.

1/2 pound hot bulk pork
    sausage or Venison
    sausage
6 slices bacon

2. Stuff each quail with 1 tablespoon sausage. Render fat from bacon by placing 6 slices bacon on a paper plate covered with paper towels. Microwave on **HIGH (100%) 2 MIN-UTES**. Wrap bacon strip around stuffed quail and secure with string.

2 gurgles white wine

3. Place a Brown-In-Bag cooking bag in a 9-inch round baking dish. Arrange quail in the bag in a circle. Pour in wine. Close end of bag with a strip of plastic wrap, leaving an opening the size of a quarter. Microwave on **HIGH (100%) 15 MINUTES**. Turn quail over inside bag after half the cooking time. Remove from bag, discard strings and bag and place quail on serving dish. Cover with foil to keep warm until serving. Goes well with Cheese Grits (Tout de Suite I page 161) and biscuits.

QUAIL AU GENIÈVRE

Quail with juniper berries

Cooking Time: 22 minutes 30 seconds
Utensils: 2-cup glass measuring cup
Paper plate
9-inch browning dish with lid
Servings: 6

1/2 ounce juniper berries (available in gourmet section of grocery store, juniper berries are best known as the basic flavoring in gin)
1/3 cup cognac

1. Soak juniper berries in cognac overnight in a jar. For quicker soaking, place berries and cognac in a 2-cup measure. Cover with plastic wrap. Bring to boil on **HIGH (100%) 45 SECONDS**. Let stand covered while preparing quail.

6 slices bacon
6 quail
Micro-Shake or an all-purpose seasoning
1 Tablespoon margarine

2. Place bacon on a paper plate covered with paper towels. Microwave on **HIGH (100%) 2 MINUTES**. Wrap bacon around breast of quail and secure with string. Preheat empty browning dish on **HIGH (100%) 4 MINUTES**. Add quail and margarine, quickly turning quail to brown all sides. Cover with lid and microwave on **HIGH (100%) 12 MINUTES**. Turn and rearrange quail in dish one time.

1/4 cup cognac
3 Tablespoons beef stock
3 Tablespoons whipping cream

3. Remove browning dish to counter top. Heat cognac in a 2-cup measure on **HIGH (100%) 30–45 SECONDS**. Pour over quail and ignite. Remove strings and transfer quail to serving dish. Add drained juniper berries, stock and cream to browning dish. Microwave on **HIGH (100%) 2–3 MINUTES** until thickened. Pour sauce over quail in serving dish. Cover to keep warm. For individual servings, quail may be placed on a toasted crouton with sauce poured over top.

ROAST WILD DUCK

canard sauvage rôti

Cooking Time: 50 Minutes
Utensils: Large microwave-safe clay pot (water soaked)
            or a large covered ceramic casserole
Servings: 4

**2 (2-lb.) wild ducks or
     4 (1-lb.) ducks
Garlic powder
Onion powder
Pepper
Cayenne pepper
Salt**

1. Clean ducks. Season inside and out with garlic powder, onion powder, pepper, and cayenne pepper. Sprinkle salt inside of cavity.

**1 apple, quartered
1 onion, quartered
4 (3-inch) pieces of celery
1 bunch of parsley**

2. Stuff each duck with apple, onion, celery and a small handful of parsley. Immerse lid and bottom of clay pot in water for 10 minutes.

**1/2 cup red wine
1 Tablespoon Kitchen
     Bouquet
1/2 cup chicken bouillon or
     broth
1 (8-oz.) can mushrooms,
     drained and sliced
1 (8-oz.) can water chestnuts,
     drained and sliced**

3. Mix wine, Kitchen Bouquet, broth, mushrooms and water chestnuts. Baste ducks all over. Place breast down in the watered clay pot and pour remaining sauce over ducks. Cover and microwave on **HIGH (100%) 20 MINUTES**. Turn ducks over and baste. Continue to cook covered on **MEDIUM (50%) 30 MINUTES**.

Delicious served with wild rice.

TEAL LA MAISON

Teal Duck cooked in a bag.

Cooking Time: 9 minutes per pound
Utensils: Round glass baking dish
      Brown-In-Bag cooking bag
      4-cup glass measuring cup
Servings: 4

4 Teal duck (2½ lbs.) cleaned
Lemon slice
Micro-Shake to sprinkle
1/2 teaspoon pepper
1/2 teaspoon paprika
1/2 teaspoon garlic powder
1 teaspoon herb seasoning
1 apple, unpeeled, quartered
    and cored
1/4 cup seasoned bread
    crumbs

1. Rub outside of duck with lemon slice. Season inside and out with Micro-Shake and then a mixture of pepper, paprika, garlic powder and herb seasoning. Stuff each duck with a quarter slice of apple. Dust lightly with seasoned bread crumbs. Place duck in a Brown-In-Bag cooking bag on a round dish (for easy removal from micro-wave).

2 Tablespoons margarine
1 cup onion, chopped
1/2 cup green bell pepper,
    chopped
1 clove garlic, chopped
3 Tablespoons Lipton dry
    onion soup mix
1/2 cup water
1 (8-oz.) can mushrooms,
    stems and pieces,
    drained

2. Micromelt margarine in a 4-cup measure on **HIGH (100%) 30 SEC-ONDS**. Add onion, bell pepper and garlic. Sauté on **HIGH (100%) 3 MINUTES**. Stir in onion soup mix, water and mushrooms. Pour mixture over duck in bag. Close end of bag with a strip of plastic, leaving an opening the size of a quarter. Microwave on **HIGH (100%) 9 MIN-UTES PER POUND**.

3 Tablespoons orange juice
1½ Tablespoons orange
    marmalade
Juice of 1/4 lemon
3 Tablespoons red wine

3. During the last 15 minutes of cooking turn ducks over in bag and add a mixture of orange juice, orange marmalade, lemon juice and red wine. Ducks are done when meat at breast bone begins to separate slightly. Serve duck and mushroom gravy with steamed rice.

VENISON ROAST II

Cooking Time: 15 minutes per pound
Utensils: Cooking bag, microsafe rack
           7 x 11-inch glass baking dish
Servings: 10 to 12

**1 (8-lb.) venison roast, weigh
  after trimming to
  estimate cooking time
3 cups milk, to marinate
1/4 cup red wine
1/4 cup Worcestershire sauce
1 Tablespoon commercial
  Liquid Smoke
1 Tablespoon Tabasco
Red pepper to sprinkle
Garlic powder to sprinkle
Micro-Shake to sprinkle**

1. Trim all membrane and gristle from roast. Pierce meat all over with a fork. Place roast in a plastic bag. Add milk to bag and marinate overnight in refrigerator. Drain. Make slits in venison and rub in a mixture of red wine, Worcestershire, Liquid Smoke and Tabasco. Sprinkle venison with red pepper, garlic powder and Micro-Shake. Place meat in a large Brown-In-Bag cooking bag. Close end of bag with a strip of plastic, leaving an opening the size of a quarter.

Place meat and bag on a rack in a 7 x 11-inch baking dish. Estimate cooking time. Microwave on **MEDIUM (50%) 15 MINUTES PER POUND**. For an 8-pound roast, cooking time would be 2 hours. Let stand in bag 10 minutes. Remove, slice and serve with Marchand de Vin Sauce.

MARCHAND DE VIN SAUCE II

Cooking Time: 14 minutes
Utensil: 4-cup glass measuring cup

**2 Tablespoons vegetable oil
2 Tablespoons flour
3/4 cup onion, finely chopped
4 green onions, tops and
  bulbs chopped
1½ cups beef stock
3 Tablespoons tomato sauce
1/3 cup red wine
Dash of lemon juice
Salt and pepper to taste**

1. Mix oil and flour together completely in a 4-cup measure to make a roux. Microwave on **HIGH (100%) 6–7 MINUTES** until brown. Add onions and microwave on **HIGH (100%) 3 MINUTES**. Stir in beef stock and tomato sauce. Microwave on **HIGH (100%) 3–4 MINUTES** until mixture boils. Add red wine and a dash of lemon juice. Season to taste with salt and pepper. Serve over sliced meat or steaks.

Meat

Meat:

carne   *Spanish*
carni   *Italian*
viandes French

Microwaving brings out the full flavor of fresh quality beef, pork, lamb and veal.

ALOUETTES SANS TÊTE

Pronounced al-OOH-et sah tet

A French recipe with veal scallops

Cooking Time: 13 minutes
Utensil: 9-inch browning dish with lid
Servings: 6

**1½ pounds (6) veal scallops,
or thin slice of veal
round cut in 6 portions
1/2 pound ham, 6 thin slices
1/2 pound Gruyère, cut in 6
chunks**

1. On a thin veal scallop, place a thin slice of ham and a chunk of cheese. Roll to enclose cheese. Secure with string or wooden picks.

**2 Tablespoons margarine
All-purpose herb seasoning
to sprinkle**

2. Preheat empty browning dish on **HIGH (100%) 4 MINUTES**. Add margarine and veal bundles, quickly turning meat to sear. Cover with lid and microwave on **HIGH (100%) 3 MINUTES**. Remove bundles from dish, sprinkle with herb seasoning and set aside covered to keep warm.

**2 Tablespoons margarine
4 Tablespoons shallots,
chopped white bulb
1/2 pound mushrooms, sliced
1/4 cup white wine
2 Tablespoons parsley,
snipped
1/2 cup dairy sour cream
1/4 teaspoon salt
1/8 teaspoon white pepper**

3. Discard liquid from dish. Add margarine, shallots and mushrooms. Sauté on **HIGH (100%) 3 MINUTES**. Add wine, parsley, sour cream, salt and pepper. Return veal bundles to dish. Cover and microwave on **HIGH (100%) 3 MINUTES**. Remove strings or picks before serving.

BEEF CORDON BLEU

boeuf cordon bleu

In five minutes

Cooking Time: 5 minutes 30 seconds
Utensil: 9-inch glass pie plate
Servings: 4

**1 pound beef sirloin steak,
sliced 1/4-inch thick**
**4 thin slices prosciutto or
ham**
**4-ounces Monterey Jack
cheese, cut in 3-inch
sticks**
**1 egg, beaten with 1
Tablespoon water**
**1/2 cup Italian seasoned
bread crumbs**

1. Trim fat from steak and divide beef into 4 pieces. Flatten beef with mallet to 1/8-inch thickness. Roll prosciutto around cheese sticks and place each bundle on a piece of beef. Fold beef over and secure with wooden picks or string. Dip meat in egg mixture then coat with crumbs.

2 Tablespoons margarine
**2 Tablespoons dry white
wine**
Snipped parsley

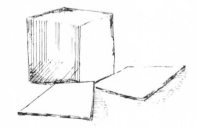

2. Melt margarine in a 9-inch glass pie plate or shallow baking dish on **HIGH (100%) 30 SECONDS**. Place beef in melted margarine and microwave uncovered on **HIGH (100%) 2 MINUTES**. Turn beef over and continue to microwave on **HIGH (100%) 3 MINUTES** or until done as desired. Rotate dish one time. Transfer beef to serving platter and remove picks or string. Add wine to remaining margarine in plate. Swirl around and drizzle over beef. Sprinkle with parsley.

To make your own seasoning-browning mix in less than 5 minutes— combine 2 Tablespoons salt, 2 teaspoons flour, 1 teaspoon paprika and 1/4 teaspoon pepper in a salt shaker. Compliments of Gay Starrak, Director of Consumer Services Department, National Live Stock and Meat Board.

BEEF ENCHILADAS

enchiladas de res molida con salsa roja

With red enchilada sauce

Cooking Time: 38 minutes 45 seconds
Utensils: 2 (4-cup) glass measuring cups
Plastic colander and 2-quart glass bowl
7 x 11-inch glass baking dish
Servings: 6

1½ pounds lean ground beef
3/4 cup onion, chopped
1½ cups Red Enchilada Sauce*
Pinch of ground cumin
1/4 cup chopped ripe olives
2 teaspoons salt

*RED ENCHILADA SAUCE:

1 teaspoon vegetable oil
1/4 cup onion, chopped
1 clove garlic, minced
2½ cups chicken broth or stock
1/4 cup flour
1¼ cups red chili sauce or an all-purpose red Mexican sauce
1 teaspoon salt
1 Tablespoon chili powder

12 soft corn tortillas
1½ cups Red Enchilada Sauce, heated
1½ cups mild Cheddar cheese, grated

1. Place meat and onion in plastic colander over a glass bowl. Cover with wax paper. Microwave on **HIGH (100%) 7 MINUTES**, stirring once or twice to break up meat. Discard drippings and return meat to bowl. Add Red Enchilada Sauce, cumin, olives and salt. Cover and microwave on **HIGH (100%) 7 MINUTES**.

2. In a 4-cup measure sauté oil, onion and garlic on **HIGH (100%) 2 MINUTES**. Add chicken broth and bring to boil on **HIGH (100%) 5 MINUTES**. Place flour in another 4-cup measure. Gradually add Mexican sauce so the flour will not lump. Add salt, chili powder and hot chicken broth. Mix well and microwave on **HIGH (100%) 7 MINUTES**. Stir at 3 minute intervals. Makes 1 quart.

3. Wrap 12 tortillas in a wet dish towel. Microwave on **HIGH (100%) 45 SECONDS**. Dip each tortilla in sauce. Divide the meat sauce evenly among tortillas. Roll and place seam side down in a greased 7 x 11-inch baking dish. Spoon any remaining sauce and meat sauce over enchiladas. Cover with wax paper. Microwave on **HIGH (100%) 7 MINUTES**. Rotate dish once. Sprinkle with cheese and continue to microwave uncovered on **HIGH (100%) 3 MINUTES**.

100

ENCHILADA PIE MARACAIBO

pastel enchilada maracaibo

Cooking Time: 21 minutes
Utensils: Plastic colander and glass pie plate
2-quart round glass casserole
7 x 11-inch glass baking dish
Servings: 6

1½ pounds lean ground beef
1/4 teaspoon chili powder
1/4 teaspoon garlic powder
1/2 teaspoon salt
1/4 teaspoon pepper

1. Place meat in a plastic colander over a pie plate to catch drippings. Cover with wax paper. Microwave on **HIGH (100%) 6 to 7 MINUTES**. Stir meat two times to break up lumps. Add chili powder, garlic powder, salt and pepper to cooked meat. Cover and let stand in colander.

3 Tablespoons flour
3 Tablespoons water
2 (10-oz.) cans enchilada sauce

2. Place flour in a 2-quart round dish, stir in water slowly to make a thin paste. Blend in enchilada sauce. Microwave on **HIGH (100%) 5 MINUTES**, stirring once.

12 soft corn tortillas*
1/2 cup ripe olives, chopped
1 cup onion, chopped
2 cups mild Cheddar cheese, grated

3. Place 6 tortillas dipped in warm enchilada sauce in bottom of a greased 7 x 11-inch glass dish. Sprinkle all the cooked meat mixture over tortillas. Layer half the olives, onion, cheese and enchilada sauce mixture. Layer remaining tortillas dipped in sauce and repeat layers of olives, onion, cheese and sauce. Cover with wax paper and microwave on **HIGH (100%) 9 MINUTES**. Turn dish at half the cooking time.

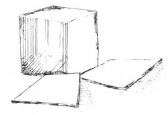

*MICRO MEMO:

To soften tortillas wrap 12 tortillas in a damp cloth dish towel. Microwave on **HIGH (100%) 45 SECONDS**.

101

BRACIOLA RIPIENA

An Italian stuffed rolled roast.

Cooking Time: 20 minutes
Utensils: 4-cup glass measuring cup
10-inch glass pie plate
5 x 9-inch glass loaf dish
Servings: 8

1½–2 pounds beef sirloin, butterflied and flattened to 1/4-inch
Micro-Shake
All-purpose herb seasoning

1. Flatten meat to approximately 10 x 13-inch shape. Season meat with Micro-Shake and an all-purpose herb seasoning.

1 Tablespoon olive oil
1/2 cup onion, chopped
1 clove garlic, minced
1 slice bacon, diced
1 (14-oz.) can artichokes, drained and chopped
2 sprigs parsley, snipped

2. Place oil, onion, garlic and bacon in a 4-cup measure. Cover and microwave on **HIGH (100%) 3 MINUTES**. Add artichokes and parsley. Microwave on **HIGH (100%) 2 MINUTES**. Set aside.

3 eggs, beaten
Herb seasoning
1–2 Tablespoons Parmesan cheese, grated
1/4 pound Italian mortadella Bologna, thinly sliced

3. Pour eggs into a buttered 10-inch pie plate to make a thin frittata. Cover with plastic wrap and microwave on **HIGH (100%) 3 MINUTES**. Stir at 1 minute (before frittata sets). Lay frittata on meat. Sprinkle with herb seasoning and Parmesan cheese. Place mortadella over all the surface. Mound artichoke mixture on top of mortadella. Roll all layers tightly, obtaining a roast-like shape. Tie roll in four places securing ends with wooden picks.

1/2 onion, quartered
1/8 teaspoon rosemary, fresh if available
1/2 cup dry red wine

4. Place onions, rosemary and wine in a 5 x 9-inch loaf dish. Place roast over onions, cover with a tent of wax paper. Microwave on **HIGH (100%) 10 to 12 MINUTES**, turning roast in dish at 3 minute intervals. Transfer the roast onto a cutting board and let stand 10 minutes. Slice carefully and place on a platter pouring the wine sauce over it. Serve immediately.

ANN'S BRISKET IN A BAG

Cooking Time: 17 to 20 minutes per pound
Utensils: Large Brown-In-Bag cooking bag
Rack and 12-inch glass plate
Servings: 10

1 beef brisket, 10–11 pounds before trimming, 7–8 pounds after trimming fat
1 teaspoon onion powder
1 teaspoon garlic powder
1 teaspoon celery salt (3 teaspoons of onion/ garlic Micro-Shake may be substituted as seasoning)
2 Tablespoons Worcestershire sauce
2 Tablespoons Liquid Barbecue Smoke
1 cup barbecue sauce

MICRO MEMO:

Brisket can marinate overnight or be cooked immediately. Meat should be at room temperature before cooking.

1. Trim all fat from brisket. If starting with a 10–11 pound brisket, expect to trim 2–3 pounds of fat. Pierce meat all over with a fork and rub a mixture of onion powder, garlic powder and celery salt into both sides of brisket. Sprinkle with Worcestershire sauce and Liquid Smoke. Use barbecue sauce later.

2. Starting with thickest end of meat, roll brisket into a uniformly rolled shape. Tie roast with string or unwaxed dental floss in 2 or 3 places to hold shape and place in Brown-In-Bag cooking bag. Weigh brisket now to figure cooking time. Close bag with plastic strip provided or cut a strip of plastic wrap to tie end of bag, leaving a hole the size of a quarter at the closing. Do not pierce bag. Place brisket on a microwave cooking grill or a rack on a 12-inch round glass plate.

3. For medium-done meat, microwave on **LOW (30%) 17 MINUTES PER POUND**. For well-done, microwave on **LOW (30%) 20 MINUTES PER POUND**. Rotate brisket inside of bag after 30 minutes cooking time. Midway through total cooking time, using baster, discard juices that have collected in bag. Add barbecue sauce and turn brisket over. Continue to microwave for remainder of cooking time. Allow 10–15 minutes standing time before removing brisket from bag.

CALABAZITA

Cooking Time: 21 minutes
Utensils: 9-inch browning dish with lid
2-quart glass casserole
Servings: 4–5

**1 pound pork chops or pork
loin, diced
2 Tablespoons onion,
chopped
1 clove garlic, minced
3 small yellow squash or 2
small zucchini, diced
unpeeled
1 teaspoon margarine**

1. Preheat empty browning dish on **HIGH (100%) 4 MINUTES**. Sear meat, turning quickly with a wooden spoon. Cover and set aside. In a 2-quart dish place onion, garlic, squash or zucchini and margarine. Cover and microwave on **HIGH (100%) 5 MINUTES**. Drain and add to meat.

**1 (16-oz.) can tomatoes,
drained
2 Tablespoons cornstarch
1/4 teaspoon cumin
1 teaspoon salt
1/4 teaspoon pepper
1 (16-oz.) can whole kernel
corn, drained**

2. Pureé tomatoes with cornstarch, cumin, salt and pepper. Stir in corn. Pour over meat and squash. Mix together. Cover with lid and microwave on **MEDIUM-HIGH (70%) 12 MINUTES**, stirring once. Chicken may be substituted for pork as a delicious variation. Serve with corn bread.

PARTY CROWN ROAST OF PORK
With apple stuffing

Cooking Time: Stuffing 5 minutes
                 Roast 17 minutes per pound
Utensils: Bacon rack tray or 7 x 11-inch glass dish
                 4-cup glass measuring cup
Servings: 8–10

1/4 cup margarine
1/2 cup onion, chopped
1 cup celery, chopped
1/2 cup raisins
3 cups apples, peeled, cored
   and chopped (sprinkle
   with lemon)
4 cups white bread cubes
2 cups water chestnuts,
   coarsely chopped
1 Tablespoon salt
1 teaspoon cinnamon
1/4 teaspoon nutmeg

8–9 pound crown pork roast
   (Butcher will form a
   pork loin roast into a
   circle, removing the
   back bone for easy
   carving. Secure roast
   with string to hold
   shape while cooking.
   Trim fat from roast and
   weigh before cooking to
   estimate cooking time.)
Micro-Shake for seasoning

1. To prepare apple stuffing micromelt margarine in a 4-cup measure on **HIGH (100%) 1 MINUTE**. Add onion and celery; sauté on **HIGH (100%) 3–4 MINUTES** until tender. Lightly toss sautéed vegetables with raisins, apples, bread cubes, water chestnuts, salt, cinnamon and nutmeg in a large mixing bowl. **Helpful hint**: Apple stuffing could be completed while roast is cooking.

2. Moisten roast with water and sprinkle liberally with Micro-Shake or a mixture of flour, paprika and white pepper. Place roast with bony ribs down and meaty portion up on a bacon rack tray or on a rack in a 7 x 11-inch baking dish. Cover with wax paper. Microwave roast on **HIGH (100%) 5 MINUTES**. Then reduce power and microwave roast on **MEDIUM (50%) 17 MINUTES PER POUND**. Rotate dish at 30 minute intervals. Baste off any accumulated liquid. When approximately 30 minutes of cooking time remains, turn roast over. Fill cavity with stuffing. Fit wax paper over stuffing to prevent excess drying. Microwave roast until internal temperature reaches 175°. Let stand 10 minutes on counter covered loosely with foil until temperature reaches 185°. Remove roast to serving plate. Slice between chops to serve.

CHEESE ENCHILADAS

enchiladas de queso con salsa de enchiladas de res

With beef enchilada sauce

Cooking Time: 30 minutes 45 seconds
Utensils: Plastic colander and glass pie plate
8-cup glass measuring cup
7 x 11-inch glass baking dish
Servings: 6

SAUCE:

**2 pounds beef chuck,
   coarsely ground
1¼ cups onion, chopped
1 clove garlic, minced**

1. Mix meat, onion and garlic and place in a plastic colander over a pie plate. Cover with wax paper. Microwave on **HIGH (100%) 8 to 10 MINUTES**, stirring at 3 minute intervals so meat will not lump.

**1 (16-oz.) can whole
   tomatoes, drained and
   chopped
4 Tablespoons chili powder
1 teaspoon salt
1/4 teaspoon cayenne pepper
1/2 teaspoon ground cumin
1 (15-oz.) can pinto beans
   and liquid
1/2 cup water**

2. Place meat mixture in an 8-cup measure. Add tomatoes, chili powder, salt, pepper and cumin. Cover with plastic wrap and microwave on **HIGH (100%) 5 MINUTES**. Stir once. In a blender pureé beans and liquid with water to make a bean gravy. Pour into meat mixture. Cover and microwave on **HIGH (100%) 10 MINUTES**.

**12 soft corn tortillas
2 cups onion, chopped
4 cups grated Cheddar
   cheese**

3. Soften 12 tortillas by wrapping in a damp dish towel. Microwave on **HIGH (100%) 45 SECONDS**. Lay tortillas flat in a greased 7 x 11-inch baking dish. Fill with onion and cheese, roll and placed seam side down. Pour 6 cups warm beef enchilada sauce over enchiladas and top with remaining cheese. Microwave on **HIGH (100%) 7 MINUTES**. For quick beef nachos, spoon remaining beef sauce over corn chips on a glass plate. Microwave on **HIGH (100%) 1 MINUTE**.

CHILI CON CARNE

¡Muy bueno!

Cooking Time: 29 minutes
Utensils: 9-inch browning dish with lid
        2-cup glass measuring cup
Servings: 6

2 quarts water
6 dried chili peppers, seeded
  (If peppers are not
  available, substitute 3
  Tablespoons Gebhardt's
  chili powder)

1. Bring 2 quarts water to boil in a large pot (in the microwave or conventionally). Boil peppers until plump and the pulp can be scraped from the skin.

1 pound round steak, cubed
1/2 pound pork, cubed
2 teaspoons margarine

2. Preheat empty browning dish on **HIGH (100%) 4 MINUTES**. Drop in 1 teaspoon margarine and quickly sear round steak, stirring and turning meat with a wooden spoon. Set meat aside. Wipe dish with a paper towel and preheat dish on **HIGH (100%) 3 MINUTES**. Add 1 teaspoon margarine and quickly sear pork. Return round steak to dish. Add pulp from peppers or substitute chili powder. Cover.

3/4 cup onion, chopped
3 cloves garlic, minced
2 Tablespoons flour
1 teaspoon cumin
2 teaspoons salt
2 cups canned tomatoes,
    drained and chopped

3. In a 2-cup measure cover and microwave onion and garlic on **HIGH (100%) 2 MINUTES**. Add to meat dish. Stir in flour, cumin, salt and tomatoes. Cover and microwave on **HIGH (100%) 10 MINUTES**. Stir and microwave on **MEDIUM (50%) 10 MINUTES**.

CHOUCROUTE A L' ALSACIENNE

Pronounced shoe-kroot ah lal-says-yen

A hearty party dish of sauerkraut, sausage and frankfurters.

Cooking Time: 40 minutes
Utensils: 5-quart ceramic casserole
         1-quart glass dish
Servings: 8

1/4 cup margarine
1/2 pound slab bacon, cut in
** 1-inch chunks**
4 large carrots, sliced in
** rounds**
2 large onions, cut in chunks

2 (1-quart) jars sauerkraut,
** squeezed and drained**
** on paper towels**
1 pound cooked sausage, cut
** in diagonal pieces**
** (Andouille, Kielbasa)**
1 pound Knockwurst, cut in
** diagonal pieces**
1 pound frankfurters, cut in
** diagonal pieces**
Bouquet garni

16 juniper berries or 1/4 cup
** gin**
1/2 cup white wine or
** Vermouth**
1/2 cup champagne or
** Vermouth**
1½ cups chicken stock or
** broth**
1 pound ham or Canadian
** bacon, sliced thickly**
8 tiny new potatoes
1/2 cup water
1/2 teaspoon salt
1 Tablespoon margarine
Carraway seeds for sprinkling

1. In a 5-quart casserole microwave margarine and bacon covered on **HIGH (100%) 2 MINUTES**. Stir in carrots and onions, cover and microwave on **HIGH (100%) 10 MINUTES**, stirring once.

2. Place sauerkraut over carrot and onion pieces; mix. Add sliced sausage, Knockwurst and frankfurters. Prepare bouquet garni and place in dish with meats. **To prepare bouquet garni:** Place small amount of celery, parsley, bay leaf, peppercorns and thyme on a cheesecloth square and tie with thread to secure.

3. Add juniper berries or gin, wine, champagne or Vermouth and chicken stock to pot. Gently mix all together. Cover and microwave on **HIGH (100%) 15 MINUTES**. Stir to mix. Lay ham or Canadian bacon slices on top. Cover and microwave on **HIGH (100%) 7 MINUTES**. Arrange and serve on a large platter. Steam potatoes, water and salt in a 1-quart dish on **HIGH (100%) 6 MINUTES**. Drain and dot with margarine. Place steamed new potatoes sprinkled with carraway seeds around platter.

HUKI LAU
Pronounced who-key-loú

Cooking Time: 12 minutes
Utensils: 9-inch browning dish with lid
2-cup glass measuring cup
Servings: 4

1 pound beef tenderloin, cut in chunks
1 Tablespoon vegetable oil

1. Preheat empty browning dish on **HIGH (100%) 5 MINUTES**. Add oil and beef chunks. Quickly sear meat turning and rearranging with a wooden spoon. Some pieces may still be pink.

1/2 large green bell pepper, sliced in strips
1/2 cup onion, cut in chunks
1/2 cup celery, cut in 1/4-inch slices
1 (8½-oz.) can water chestnuts, sliced
1 (10½-oz.) can beef consommé, undiluted, (to be divided)
1/2 teaspoon garlic powder

2. Stir in bell pepper, onion, celery and water chestnuts. Pour 3/4 cup consommé (reserve remaining consommé for sauce) and garlic powder over mixture. Cover and microwave on **HIGH (100%) 5 MINUTES**, stirring once. Do not over cook meat.

SAUCE:

Remaining consommé (5 oz.)
2 Tablespoons cornstarch
1 teaspoon molasses or honey
2 teaspoon red wine
1 teaspoon salt

3. Place cornstarch in a 2-cup measure and pour remaining consommé in slowly to blend. Add honey, wine and salt. Microwave on **HIGH (100%) 2 MINUTES**, stirring at 30-second intervals. Spread sauce over meat and vegetable mixture. Serve at once with steamed rice and Chinese fried noodles.

HAM ASPARAGUS AU GRATIN

jambon aux asperges au gratin

Cooking Time: 28 minutes (plus cooking time for rice)
Utensils: 8-cup glass measuring bowl
        7 x 11-inch glass baking dish
Servings: 8

1⅓ cup cooked rice

1. Warm frozen rice in plastic bag or cook rice in a 4-quart dish according to directions on page 133.

2 (10-oz.) cartons frozen slender asparagus spears (approximately 24–32)

WHITE SAUCE:

2. Remove outer waxed wrapper and place both cartons of asparagus on a microwave safe plate. Cook on **HIGH (100%) 12 MINUTES**. Drain, trim hard stems and set aside covered.

4 Tablespoons butter
4 Tablespoons flour
3/4 teaspoon salt
2 cups milk
1 cup Swiss cheese, shredded

3. In an 8-cup measure melt butter on **HIGH (100%) 1 MINUTE**. Stir in flour and salt. Add milk gradually. Cook on **HIGH (100%) 8 MINUTES**, stirring at 3 minute intervals for the first 6 minutes and every 30 seconds until thickened. Stir in cheese until melted.

8 slices cooked ham, 1/4-inch thick
1/4 cup Parmesan cheese, grated

4. Mix together 1 cup of white sauce and 1⅓ cups cooked rice. Spoon 2 tablespoons of rice mixture onto the narrow end of ham slices. Lay 3 or 4 asparagus spears on top of rice mixture and roll ham around filling. Secure with wooden picks. Arrange rolls in a 7 x 11-inch baking dish. Pour remaining sauce over all. Sprinkle with Parmesan cheese. Cover with wax paper and microwave on **HIGH (100%) 7 MINUTES**, turning dish once.

HAM AND YAM LOUISIANE

Cooking Time: 11 minutes 40 seconds
Utensils: Mixing bowl
         4-cup glass measuring cup
         1-quart round glass casserole
Servings: 4–6

2 (17-oz.) cans yams
1/2 cup milk
2 Tablespoons margarine,
** melted**
1 teaspoon salt

2 Tablespoons margarine
1/4 cup onion, minced
1/3 cup green bell pepper,
** diced**

1/2 pound cooked ham,
** chopped**
2 Tablespoons seedless
** raisins**

1. Drain yams, place in a mixing bowl and mash. Add milk, melted margarine and salt. Beat until light and fluffy.

2. In a 4-cup measure, micromelt margarine on **HIGH (100%) 40 SECONDS**. Stir in onion and green pepper and microwave on **HIGH (100%) 1 MINUTE**. Add ham and raisins, cover with plastic wrap and microwave on **HIGH (100%) 3 MINUTES**.

3. Fold ham mixture into yam mixture and turn into a greased 1-quart round casserole. Microwave on **HIGH (100%) 7 MINUTES**.

ROAST LEG OF LAMB
With Herbs

gigot de mouton rôti

Cooking Time: See Chart*
Utensils: 1 Brown-In-Bag cooking bag
      Shallow 9-inch glass dish
Servings: 8

1 (5–7 lb.) boned leg of lamb
8 to 10 small garlic cloves
1/2 teaspoon ground thyme
1 teaspoon ground rosemary
1/2 teaspoon freshly ground
    black pepper
2 Tablespoons flour

2 Tablespoons tarragon
    vinegar
1 Tablespoon water

1. Trim fat from lamb. Peel garlic cloves and insert randomly into lamb, using point of sharp knife. Mix together thyme, rosemary, pepper and flour. Rub this mixture well into lamb. Roll meat and tie with string.

2. Sprinkle or pat on lamb, a mixture of tarragon vinegar and water. Place meat inside a cooking bag dusted with 1 tablespoon of flour. Close end loosely with plastic strip leaving a small opening. Do not slit bag as juices will run out.

3. Place lamb in bag in a shallow 9-inch dish. Microwave on **MEDIUM (50%) 10 MINUTES PER POUND**.* See Chart. Turn roast over after half the cooking time. Let roast stand in its juices until served. Slice and serve with green mint-flavored apple jelly or Gravy For Lamb With Herbs page 113 or Lemon Caper Sauce page 113.

CHART FOR LAMB

	Time Per Pound MEDIUM (50%) POWER	Temp. Before Standing Time	Temp. After Standing Time
Medium	10 min. (50%)	140°	150°
Well-done	12 min. (50%)	150°	160°

BROWN GRAVY

For lamb with herbs

Cooking Time: 5 minutes 30 seconds
Utensil: 4-cup glass measuring cup

2 Tablespoons margarine
1½ Tablespoons flour
1 cup reserved liquid from
    cooking bag (page 112)
1 (10½-oz.) can beef bouillon,
    undiluted
2–4 Tablespoons dry red
    wine
Dash freshly ground black
    pepper

1. Micromelt margarine in a 4-cup measure on **HIGH (100%) 30 SECONDS**. Stir in flour to blend. Add liquid from cooking bag and bouillon. Mix well and microwave on **HIGH (100%) 5 MINUTES** until slightly thickened, stirring twice. Stir in wine and pepper.

LEMON CAPER SAUCE

Cooking Time: 4 minutes 30 seconds
Utensil: 2-cup glass measuring cup

3 egg yolks
2 Tablespoons lemon juice
1 Tablespoon arrowroot
1/8 teaspoon salt
1/8 teaspoon cayenne pepper
1 cup chicken broth
1 rounded Tablespoon capers

1. Whisk egg yolks, lemon juice, arrowroot, salt and pepper in a 2-cup measure. Add chicken broth. Microwave on **HIGH (100%) 4 MINUTES 30 SECONDS** until thickened. Stir at 30 second intervals after the first 2 minutes. Just before serving add capers.

LASAGNA BOLOGNESE

Pasta cooks by layering with sauce.

Cooking Time: 49 minutes
Utensils: 8-cup glass measuring cup
      Plastic colander and glass pie plate
      7 x 11-inch glass baking dish
Servings: 8

BOLOGNESE SAUCE:

3 Tablespoons butter
1⅔ cup onion, finely chopped
3/4 cup carrots, finely chopped
1/2 cup celery, finely chopped
2 cloves garlic, minced

1. Melt butter in an 8-cup measure on **HIGH (100%) 1 MINUTE**. Add onion, carrots, celery and garlic. Cover with plastic wrap. Microwave on **HIGH (100%) 10–12 MINUTES**, until vegetables soften, stirring twice. Cover and set aside.

3/4 pound lean pork, ground
3/4 pound lean beef, ground
1½ teaspoons salt
1/2 teaspoon each basil, sage and oregano
1/4 teaspoon white pepper
Freshly ground black pepper
Freshly grated nutmeg

2. Combine pork and beef. Place in a plastic colander over a pie plate, to catch drippings. Cover with wax paper and microwave on **HIGH (100%) 8 MINUTES**, stirring twice to break up lumps. Add meat to sautéed vegetables. Stir in salt, basil, sage, oregano, pepper and nutmeg.

1 (10¾-oz.) can tomato purée
2 Tablespoons tomato paste
1½ cups beef broth or stock
1/2 cup dry white wine

3. Add tomato purée, tomato paste, stock and wine to meat mixture. Cover and microwave on **HIGH (100%) 8 MINUTES** until thickened, stirring twice. Prepare Béchamel Sauce on page 115.

(Continued on next page)

LASAGNA BOLOGNESE (Continued)

TO ASSEMBLE:

1 (8-oz.) package Lasagna, green or white, uncooked (dip in warm water just before layering)
1 cup Parmesan cheese, grated

4. Spread 1 cup Bolognese meat sauce on bottom of greased 7 x 11-inch baking dish. Place alternate layers of uncooked pasta, Bolognese sauce, Béchamel sauce* and Parmesan cheese. Repeat in this order until all ingredients have been used, ending with a layer of Parmesan cheese. Press down gently with spoon to be sure all noodles (pasta) are moistened. Insert 3 or 4 wooden picks in top of Lasagna to hold a covering of wax paper above cheese. Microwave on **HIGH (100%) 10 MINUTES**. Rotate dish 1/2 turn. Continue to microwave on **HIGH (100%) 10 MINUTES** or until noodles are tender.

*BÉCHAMEL SAUCE

Cooking Time: 8 minutes
Utensils: 2-cup glass measuring cup
4-cup glass measuring cup
Servings: Makes 2 cups

2 cups milk, hot
4 Tablespoons butter
4 Tablespoons flour
1 teaspoon salt
1/4 teaspoon white pepper

Heat milk in a 2-cup measure on **HIGH (100%) 4 MINUTES**. Melt butter in a 4-cup measure on **HIGH (100%) 1 MINUTE**. Add flour, salt, pepper and slowly blend in hot milk. Microwave on **HIGH (100%) 3 MINUTES**, stirring at 1 minute intervals.

CANNELLONI WITH RICOTTA
cannelloni alla ricotta

Cooking Time: 21 minutes
Utensils: 2-quart glass casserole
            7 x 11-inch glass baking dish
Servings: 6

SAUCE:

1 Tablespoon olive oil
1 cup onion, chopped
1 carrot, chopped
1 stalk celery, chopped
1 (1 lb. 12-oz.) can whole
   tomatoes, drained and
   puréed in food
   processor
1/2 teaspoon salt
1/8 teaspoon pepper
1/8 teaspoon nutmeg

1. Sauté oil, onion, carrot and celery in a 2-quart casserole covered with plastic wrap or tight fitting lid on **HIGH (100%) 5 MINUTES**, stirring once. Add tomatoes, salt, pepper and nutmeg. Cover and microwave on **HIGH (100%) 10 MINUTES**, stirring once. Set aside covered.

12 large cannelloni or
   manicotti pasta

2. Boil pasta *al dente* in microwave or use conventional method according to package directions. Drain.

STUFFING:

1 cup Mozzarella cheese,
   grated
1½ cups cooked ham, diced
12 ounces Ricotta cheese
2 eggs
1/8 teaspoon nutmeg
1 teaspoon salt
1/2 teaspoon pepper
1/2 teaspoon basil
Parmesan cheese to sprinkle
1 Tablespoon melted butter

3. Combine cheese, ham, Ricotta, eggs, nutmeg, salt and pepper in a mixing bowl. Stuff pasta with ham mixture and place in a buttered 7 x 11-inch baking dish. Pour sauce over cannelloni. Sprinkle with basil, Parmesan cheese and butter. Microwave on **HIGH (100%) 6 MINUTES** until cheese melts on top.

MANICOTTI ORIN

Cooking Time: 16 minutes
Utensils: 7 x 11-inch glass baking dish
         Plastic colander and a 2-quart glass bowl
Servings: 6

1 (8-oz.) package 12–14 manicotti shells

1. Follow package directions for cooking pasta. Drain.

STUFFING:

1 (10-oz.) carton frozen chopped spinach, defrosted
1 (12-oz.) carton dry cottage cheese
1 egg, slightly beaten
2 Tablespoons seasoned bread crumbs
1 cup Parmesan cheese, grated
1 teaspoon salt
1/8 teaspoon pepper

2. Squeeze spinach dry and mix in a bowl with cottage cheese, egg, bread crumbs, Parmesan cheese, salt and pepper. Blend well and stuff manicotti shells with mixture. Place stuffed shells in a 7 x 11-inch baking dish. Prepare sauce.

SAUCE:

1/2 pound ground round beef
1 cup onion, chopped
1 (1½-oz.) package Lawry's spaghetti sauce mix
1 (8-oz.) can tomato sauce
1 (4-oz.) can whole mushrooms, drained and cut in half

3. Place meat and onion in a plastic colander over a 2-quart glass mixing bowl. Cover with wax paper. Microwave on **HIGH (100%) 4 MINUTES**, stirring once to break up lumps. Discard liquid and transfer meat to bowl. Add spaghetti sauce mix, tomato sauce and mushrooms. Microwave on **HIGH (100%) 5 MINUTES**, stirring once.

3 large thin slices Mozzarella cheese

4. Place cheese slices over stuffed shells. Pour sauce over cheese and microwave on **HIGH (100%) 7 MINUTES**.

MEXICANA CASSEROLE

cacerola mexicana

Cooking Time: 18 minutes
Utensils: Plastic colander
         Glass mixing bowl
         7 x 11-inch glass baking dish
Servings: 6

1 pound lean ground beef
1 teaspoon onion powder
1 teaspoon garlic powder
2 teaspoons chili powder
1/2 teaspoon salt

1. Place meat seasoned with onion powder, garlic powder and chili powder in a plastic colander over a mixing bowl. Cover with wax paper. Microwave on **HIGH (100%) 5 MINUTES**, stirring once or twice to break up meat. Add salt after cooking. Discard liquid, wipe bowl clean and return meat to bowl.

1 (16-oz.) can stewed
    tomatoes, chopped
1 (15-oz.) can ranch style
    beans, drained

2. Add stewed tomatoes and drained beans. Cover. Microwave on **HIGH (100%) 5 MINUTES**. Stir once.

1 egg
1 cup American or Cheddar
    cheese, grated
1 (8-oz.) carton cottage
    cheese

3. Mix egg, cheese and cottage cheese together in a bowl.

4 ounces slightly crushed
    tortilla chips
8–10 whole tortilla chips
1 cup American or Cheddar
    cheese, grated

4. In a 7 x 11-inch baking dish, spread half of the meat mixture; top with all the egg and cheese mixture and crushed chips. Cover with remaining meat. Place 8–10 whole tortilla chips over meat and top with grated cheese. Microwave on **HIGH (100%) 8 MINUTES**, rotating dish once.

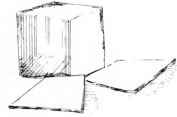

MEXICAN STACK-UP

escalera mexicana

Cooking Time: 14 minutes
Utensils: Plastic colander and 2-quart glass bowl
　　　　　10 x 10-inch ceramic baking dish
Servings: 8

1½ pounds lean ground beef
1 (1¼-oz.) package dry taco
**　seasoning**
1 teaspoon chili powder

1. Place meat in a plastic colander over a 2-quart bowl. Cover with wax paper and microwave on **HIGH (100%) 7 MINUTES**, stirring at 2 minute intervals to break up lumps. Discard drippings and place meat in bowl. Add dry taco seasoning and chili powder to meat.

1 (23-oz.) can ranch style
**　beans (pinto), drained**
1/4 cup taco sauce, hot or
**　mild**

2. Purée drained beans in food processor with steel blade or use blender. Add taco sauce and process until smooth.

2 large flour tortillas
1 cup onion, chopped
1/2 cup taco sauce, hot or
**　mild**
2 cups mild Cheddar cheese,
**　grated**

3. Place 1 tortilla in a 10 x 10-inch baking dish. Layer half the meat, beans, onion, taco sauce and cheese. Repeat layers over second tortilla ending with cheese on top. Microwave on **HIGH (100%) 7 MIN- UTES**. Slice in wedges and serve warm.

SAVORY EYE OF ROUND

Cooking Time: 13 minutes per pound 50% power
Internal temperature 140°
Utensils: 7 x 11-inch glass baking dish
Brown-In-Bag (6-pound size)
Servings: 6–8

3–3½ pound beef eye of round
Micro-Shake
1 teaspoon flour

1. Trim fat and gristle from beef. Puncture meat with fork. Sprinkle with Micro-Shake if available. (This helps to tenderize the meat.) Do not sprinkle salt on meat. Dust inside of the Brown-In-Bag with flour. Place bag in a 7 x 11-inch baking dish.

1 (10¾-oz.) can cream of celery soup, undiluted
1 (1⅜-oz.) package dry onion soup mix

2. Spoon celery soup into Brown-In-Bag cooking bag. Pat one half package dry onion soup mix on meat and sprinkle remainder in bag. Place meat on top of soup and rotate meat to coat. Close bag with plastic strip leaving a hole the size of a quarter at the closing. Do not pierce bag. If a probe is used, insert in this opening.

For Temperature Cooking with probe:

3. Microwave on **MEDIUM (50%)** to reach an internal temperature of 140° (Medium Well Done). Remember the internal temperature will increase 10° to 15° while standing. Do not overcook. Rotate meat in bag one time.

For Time Cooking:

Microwave on **MEDIUM (50%) 13 MINUTES PER POUND**. Use a microwave-safe thermometer to check internal temperature of 140° for Medium Well Done. Rotate meat inside bag after half the cooking time. Allow 10–15 minutes standing time before removing meat from bag. Slice thinly and pour warm gravy over meat.

SICILIAN LOAF

carne tritata alla siciliana

Cooking Time: 20 minutes
Utensil: 7 x 11-inch glass baking dish
Servings: 8

2 eggs, beaten
3/4 cup soft bread crumbs
1/2 cup tomato juice
2 Tablespoons parsley
3/4 teaspoon oregano
1½ teaspoons salt
1/2 teaspoon red pepper
1 clove garlic, minced
2 pounds lean ground beef
8 thin slices cooked ham
6 ounces Mozzarella cheese,
    grated

1. In a large bowl combine eggs, bread crumbs, tomato juice, parsley, oregano, salt, pepper and garlic. Add meat and mix well. On a large piece of foil pat and shape meat into 10 x 12-inch rectangle. Arrange ham slices on top of meat leaving 1-inch borders around edges. Sprinkle cheese over ham. Roll meatloaf by starting on short side. Lift foil until meat begins to roll tightly. Peel back foil and continue to lift and peel until roll is formed. Seal edges and ends. Remove from foil and place in a greased 7 x 11-inch baking dish seam side down. Microwave on **HIGH (100%) 18 MINUTES**. Rotate dish one time.

3 slices Mozzarella cheese,
    cut in half-triangle
    shape

2. Place cheese on top and microwave on **HIGH (100%) 2 MINUTES**. Let stand 5 minutes before serving.

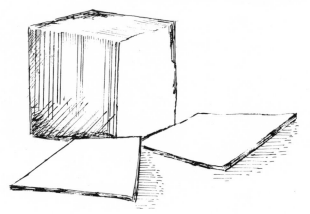

121

SPAGHETTI SALERNO

spaghetti alla salernitana

Cooking Time: 22 minutes
Utensils: Bacon rack
        4-cup glass measuring cup
        Plastic colander, 4-quart glass mixing bowl
        7 x 11-inch glass baking dish
Servings: 8

6 slices bacon
3 Tablespoons hot bacon fat
1 cup onion, minced
3/4 cup green bell pepper,
    minced
1 cup mushrooms, sliced,
    canned or fresh

1. Place bacon on a rack. Cover with wax paper and microwave on **HIGH (100%) 5 MINUTES** or until bacon is crisp. Crumble and set aside for garnish. Reserve bacon fat. In a 4-cup measure microwave bacon fat, onion and peppers on **HIGH (100%) 3 MINUTES**. Add mushrooms and microwave on **HIGH (100%) 1 MINUTE**. Set aside.

1 (8-oz.) package #4
    spaghetti, broken in
    thirds

2. Prepare spaghetti according to package directions. This may be cooked conventionally while preparing step #3. Drain and set aside covered.

1 pound lean ground beef
2 cups canned tomatoes,
    drained
1 teaspoon sugar
2 teaspoons salt
1/4 teaspoon red pepper

3. Place meat in a plastic colander over a large mixing bowl to catch drippings. Cover with wax paper. Microwave on **HIGH (100%) 5 MIN-UTES**. Stir at 2½ minutes to break up lumps. Discard meat drippings and place meat in bowl. Add the onion mixture, tomatoes, sugar, salt, pepper and cooked spaghetti. Mix together well.

2 cups sharp Cheddar cheese,
    grated
Parsley

4. Grease a 7 x 11-inch baking dish heavily with bacon fat. Pour mixture into dish and top with grated cheese. Microwave on **HIGH (100%) 8 MINUTES** turning dish one time. Garnish with crisp bacon and parsley.

STUFFED FLANK STEAK
Todd's favorite

Cooking Time: 11 minutes
Utensils: 4-cup glass measuring cup
1-cup glass measuring cup
Trivet and shallow glass baking dish
Servings: 4–6

1 (2-lb.) beef flank steak
1 teaspoon salt
1/4 teaspoon pepper
1/4 teaspoon parsley, minced
1/4 teaspoon basil, dried
1/4 teaspoon marjoram, dried

1. Pound steak to 1/2-inch thickness. Score meat diagonally on both sides. Mix together salt, pepper, parsley, basil and marjoram. Sprinkle on one side of meat.

1/4 cup margarine
1/2 pound fresh mushrooms, sliced
2 Tablespoons green onions and tops, sliced thinly
1/2 cup seasoned bread crumbs

2. Micromelt margarine in a 4-cup measure on **HIGH (100%) 1 MINUTE**. Add mushrooms and onions. Sauté on **HIGH (100%) 3 MINUTES**. Stir in bread crumbs. Spread mixture over surface of meat leaving a 1-inch margin at edges. Starting at the narrow end, roll steak, jelly-roll fashion. Tie with string at 1-inch intervals or secure edge with wooden picks. Place rolled steak on a rack or trivet in a shallow dish.

1/4 cup Worcestershire sauce
1/4 cup margarine

3. Heat Worcestershire sauce and margarine in a 1-cup measure on **HIGH (100%) 1 MINUTE**. Baste top of meat with mixture. Cover with a tent of wax paper. Microwave on **HIGH (100%) 6 MINUTES**. Turn meat over a quarter of a turn every 2 minutes and baste generously with mixture. Remove string or picks. Slice into 1/2-inch thick slices.

STUFFED GRAPE LEAVES

foglie di uva ripiene

Cooking Time: 15 minutes
Utensils: Large bowl
　　　　　Mixing bowl
　　　　　7 x 11-inch glass baking dish
Servings: Makes 32

32 grape leaves
1 teaspoon salt

1. Place leaves in a large bowl of salted hot water until limp (about 15 minutes).

1 pound lean ground beef
1 cup cooked rice
1 egg
1/2 cup onion, chopped
1/2 cup tomato sauce
2 Tablespoons parsley,
　　chopped
1 teaspoon salt
1/8 teaspoon allspice
1/4 teaspoon Cavender's
　　Greek seasoning
1/4 cup butter, melted
Juice of one lemon

2. In a mixing bowl combine beef, rice, egg, onion, tomato sauce, parsley, salt, allspice and Cavender's Greek seasoning. Place 1 heaping tablespoon of meat in center of each leaf and fold leaves over meat. Arrange in rows in a 7 x 11-inch baking dish. Drizzle with melted butter and lemon juice. Cover with plastic wrap and microwave on **HIGH (100%) 15 MINUTES**. Rotate dish one time.

The grape leaves are tender, flavorful and edible. Stuffed Grape Leaves may be prepared ahead, refrigerated and microwaved just before serving.

TAMALE PIE

pastel de tamales

Cooking Time: 35 minutes
Utensils: 4-cup glass measuring cup
          Plastic colander and 3-quart glass bowl
          7 x 11-inch glass baking dish
Servings: 8

3 cups water
1½ teaspoons salt
1 cup yellow corn meal

1. In a 4-cup measure bring water and salt to boil on **HIGH (100%) 6 MINUTES**. Stir in corn meal slowly until well blended. Microwave on **HIGH (100%) 1 MINUTE** to thicken. Spread corn meal mixture over bottom and sides of greased 7 x 11-inch baking dish. Microwave on **HIGH (100%) 10 MINUTES**. Set aside.

1 pound lean ground beef
1 cup onion, chopped
1 clove garlic, minced

2. Place meat, onion and garlic in plastic colander over a 3-quart bowl. Cover with wax paper. Microwave on **HIGH (100%) 7 MINUTES**, stirring twice. Discard fat and place meat in bowl.

1½ cups whole kernel corn,
    drained
1 (4-oz.) can whole green
    chilies, seeded and
    chopped
2 cups whole tomatoes,
    drained and chopped
1½ Tablespoons flour
3 Tablespoons chili powder
1 teaspoon salt
1/4 teaspoon red pepper
1/4 teaspoon cumin
1/2 cup ripe olives, chopped
1½ cups Cheddar cheese,
    grated

3. Add corn, chilies, tomatoes, flour, chili powder, salt, pepper, cumin and olives to meat. Mix well and pour into corn meal crust. Sprinkle with cheese and microwave on **HIGH (100%) 11 MINUTES**, rotating dish once.

125

Dressings/Rice

Eggs / Bread

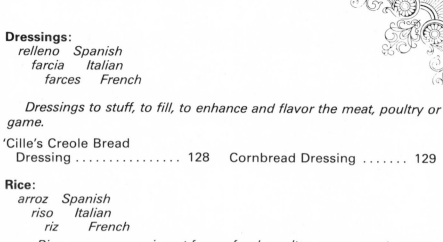

Dressings:
relleno   Spanish
farcia   Italian
farces   French

Dressings to stuff, to fill, to enhance and flavor the meat, poultry or game.

Rice:
arroz   Spanish
riso   Italian
riz   French

Rice, an accompaniment for seafood, poultry, game, meat, soups, vegetables, gumbo and even dessert, is low in fat and high in nutritional value.

Eggs:
huevos   Spanish
nova   Italian
oeufs   French

The all purpose egg binds, leavens, or thickens much of our cooking and baking yet offers itself to us for hearty breakfasts, light lunches or elegant dinners.

Bread:
pan   Spanish
pane   Italian
pains   French

The microwave fast-rising method makes warm homemade bread fun to serve.

'CILLE'S CREOLE BREAD DRESSING

farce au pain creole 'cille

Topped with toasted pecans

Cooking Time: 21 minutes
Utensils: 2-quart glass dish
             1-cup glass measuring cup
Servings: 8

1/4 cup margarine
1 pound Swift or Owen Hot Sausage
1 cup celery, diced
2 cups onions, chopped
1/2 cup green bell pepper, chopped

1. In a 2-quart dish melt margarine on **HIGH (100%) 1 MINUTE**. Add sausage, celery, onion and bell pepper. Stir to mix. Cover. Microwave on **HIGH (100%) 10 MINUTES** stirring every 3 minutes. Do not drain.

1 (7-oz.) box herb seasoned croutons
1 cup milk

2. Add croutons. Toss lightly to mix. Place milk in a 1-cup measure and microwave on **HIGH (100%) 2 MINUTES**. Pour over mixture to dampen croutons.

1 cup pecan halves, toasted

3. Cover top with toasted* pecan halves. Microwave on **HIGH (100%) 8 MINUTES** or until hot throughout. May be prepared in advance, refrigerated and baked when ready for use. Freezes beautifully.

MICRO MEMO:

** To toast pecans place 1 cup of pecans on a plate or paper plate. Microwave on **HIGH (100%) 2–4 MINUTES**.*

CORNBREAD DRESSING

farce au pain de maïs

For roast chicken

Cooking Time: 13 minutes
Utensils: 5 x 9-inch glass loaf dish
  4-cup glass measuring cup
  1-quart glass casserole
Servings: Makes 4 cups

**1 (6-oz.) package yellow
  cornbread mix
1 egg, slightly beaten
2/3 cup milk**

1. In a 1-quart bowl stir cornbread mix, egg and milk together with a fork. Pour into a greased 5 x 9-inch loaf dish. Microwave on **HIGH (100%) 5–6 MINUTES**. Crumble into a 3-quart mixing bowl.

**1/4 cup margarine
1/2 cup green onion tops and
  bulbs, chopped
1 cup celery, chopped
1/2 cup parsley, chopped
2 slices of dry bread,
  crumbled
2 eggs, beaten
1 teaspoon poultry seasoning
1 teaspoon salt
1/4 teaspoon pepper
2 hard-cooked eggs, chopped
1/4–1/2 cup chicken stock or
  bouillon**

2. Melt margarine in a 4-cup measure on **HIGH (100%) 1 MINUTE**. Stir in onions, celery and parsley. Sauté on **HIGH (100%) 3 MINUTES**. Add sautéed vegetables, bread, eggs, poultry seasoning, salt, pepper and chopped eggs to crumbled cornbread. Stir in enough stock or bouillon to moisten the dressing. Stuff a 3-pound chicken with dressing and follow directions for Roast Chicken on page 86. Place any extra dressing in a 1-quart casserole and microwave on **HIGH (100%) 3 MINUTES**.

GREEN RICE
arroz verde

Cooking Time: 22 minutes
Utensils: 4-quart ceramic casserole
Servings: 6

3 cups water
1½ teaspoons salt
1½ cups long grain rice

1. Bring 3 cups of water to a boil in a 4-quart casserole on **HIGH (100%) 7 MINUTES**. Add salt and rice. Stir and cover with wax paper. Microwave on **HIGH (100%) 5 MINUTES**.

6 whole green chilies, seeded and chopped
3 Tablespoons parsley, chopped
1 clove garlic, minced
Dash freshly ground black pepper

2. Add green chilies, parsley, garlic and pepper. Cover. Microwave on **HIGH (100%) 10 MINUTES** or until liquid is absorbed. Stir at 5 minute intervals.

This rice may be served with Shrimp Veracruz on page 67 and may be used as a side dish for other Mexican dishes.

MICRO MEMO:

Freeze leftover cooked rice in a plastic bag for future reheating. Measure rice and mark bag before freezing. Thaw and reheat in one step. Place slightly opened bag on a plate and microwave on **HIGH (100%)** *1–2 minutes per cup rice.*

MEXICAN RICE WITH TOMATOES

arroz con jitomate a la mexicana

Pronounced ah-RROS con hee-toe-MAH-teh

Cooking Time: 23 minutes
Utensils: 4-cup glass measuring cup
         9-inch browning dish with lid
Servings: 6

1 cup raw rice
2 cups water

1. Bring rice and water to a boil in a 4-cup measure covered with plastic wrap on **HIGH (100%) 3½–4 MINUTES**. Let sit covered 5 to 10 minutes until rice swells. Drain in a colander.

1 Tablespoon vegetable oil
1 cup onion, chopped
2 cloves garlic, minced
1 (4-oz.) can whole green chilies, seeded and chopped large OR 2 chilies serranos, seeded and quartered
1 cup canned tomatoes, chopped, reserve liquid
1/2 cup reserved liquid from tomatoes
1/2 cup chicken stock
1 teaspoon salt
1/4 teaspoon pepper
1 teaspoon ground cumin
1 teaspoon chili powder

2. Preheat empty browning dish on **HIGH (100%) 4 MINUTES**. Quickly add oil and rice stirring with a wooden spoon so rice will not burn. Add onion, garlic, chilies, tomatoes, juice, stock, salt, pepper, cumin and chili powder. Cover with lid and microwave on **HIGH (100%) 15 MINUTES**, stirring twice. Let stand covered 10 minutes.

RICE DRESSING

farce au riz

Better known as "Dirty Rice"

Cooking Time: 21 minutes
Utensils: Plastic colander and glass bowl
4-quart glass bowl
Servings: Makes 3 quarts

4 cups cooked long grain rice

1. Prepare rice your favorite way or use directions on page 133.

2 pounds ground beef
2 teaspoons Creole seasoning (or your favorite seasoning)

2. Place meat in a plastic colander over a glass bowl. Cover with wax paper. Microwave on **HIGH (100%) 7–8 MINUTES** until all meat is cooked. Stir two times. Discard liquid. Sprinkle Creole seasoning on meat. Set aside covered in colander.

1/4 cup margarine
2 cups onions, chopped
2/3 cup green bell pepper, chopped
1/2 cup celery, chopped
1/2 cup parsley, chopped
4 cloves garlic, minced

3. Micromelt margarine in a 4-quart bowl on **HIGH (100%) 1 MINUTE**. Add onions, bell pepper, celery, parsley and garlic. Cover and sauté on **HIGH (100%) 7 MINUTES**, stirring once.

1 teaspoon concentrated beef flavored base, (Bovril or Kitchen Bouquet)
1 cup beef broth soup, undiluted
1½ teaspoons salt
1/4 teaspoon pepper
1/2 teaspoon red pepper
1 teaspoon Trappey's Chef-Magic Kitchen Seasoning
1 cup green onion tops, finely sliced

4. Stir in beef flavored base and beef broth. Add salt, pepper, red pepper and Trappey's Kitchen seasoning. Add meat, cooked rice and green onion tops. Toss lightly to mix. Microwave on **HIGH (100%) 4–5 MINUTES** until heated through. Serve as a side dish with game, beef, pork or poultry.

STEAMED RICE

Cooking Time: 25–30 minutes
Utensils: 4-quart ceramic casserole
Yields: 6 cups cooked rice

4 cups water
2 cups long grain rice
1 teaspoon salt

Bring water to a boil in a 4-quart casserole on **HIGH (100%) 8–10 MINUTES**. Add rice and salt. Cover with wax paper and microwave on **HIGH (100%) 15–20 MINUTES**, stirring at 10 minute intervals until rice is light and fluffy. Let stand 10 minutes.

RICE CHILI VERDE
arroz chile verde

Cooking Time: 12 minutes
Utensils: 4-cup glass measuring cup
          7 x 11-inch glass baking dish
Servings: 10

4½ cups cooked rice

1. Cook rice your favorite way or follow directions on page 133.

3 cups dairy sour cream, room temperature
1 (4-oz.) can whole green chilies, drained, seeded and chopped
1 pound Monterey Jack cheese, sliced thin

2. Mix sour cream and chilies in a 4-cup measure. Layer half of the cooked rice in a greased 7 x 11-inch baking dish. Spread half of the Jack cheese slices and half of the sour cream mixture over rice. Repeat layers ending with sour cream mixture. Microwave on **MEDIUM (50%) 11 MINUTES**, turn dish at 5 minutes.

1 cup cheddar cheese, grated

3. Sprinkle with cheddar cheese and microwave on **MEDIUM (50%) 1 MINUTE**.

MACARONI AND CHEESE

maccheroni con formaggio

A speedy stir-together dish.

Cooking Time: 11 minutes
Utensil: 2-quart glass casserole
Servings: 4

**1½ cups uncooked macaroni,
    #24 large elbow**
**1 Tablespoon dehydrated
    chopped onion**
**1½ Tablespoons all-purpose
    flour**
**1 Tablespoon pimiento,
    chopped**
1 teaspoon salt
2 cups water
**1/3 cup instant dry milk
    powder**
2 Tablespoons margarine
1 teaspoon paprika

**1¼ cups processed Old
    English Cheddar cheese,
    shredded**

1. In a 2-quart casserole combine dry macaroni, onion, flour, pimiento, salt, water, dry milk, margarine and paprika. Cover with a tight-fitting lid or plastic wrap. Microwave on **HIGH (100%) 5–6 MINUTES** until mixture boils. Stir and let stand covered 5 minutes.

2. Stir in cheese, cover and microwave on **MEDIUM-HIGH (70%) 5 MINUTES**. Stir then let stand covered 5 minutes before serving.

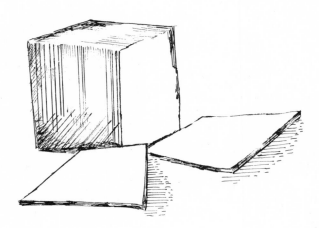

CHEESE AND MUSHROOM OMELET

frittata con formaggio e funghi

Cooking Time: 2 minutes 30 seconds
Utensils: 1-quart glass bowl
Servings: 1–2

3 large eggs, well beaten
3 Tablespoons water
2 (3/4-oz.) slices American
    processed cheese
4 fresh mushrooms, sliced
    (can be omitted)

1. In a 1-quart bowl whisk eggs then add water. Beat until mixed well. Break cheese slices into small pieces and add to egg mixture. Stir in sliced mushrooms, if desired.

2. Microwave on **HIGH (100%) 2 MINUTES 30 SECONDS**. Rotate (but do not stir) dish 1/4 turn after half the cooking time. Turn quickly out on serving plate.

CHILES RELLENOS DEL SOLOMAR

From Padre Island

Cooking Time: 10 minutes
Utensil: 1½-quart glass casserole
Servings: 6

3/4 cup half and half cream
2 eggs
1/3 cup flour

1. Whisk cream with eggs and add slowly to flour in a small bowl until smooth. Blender or food processor may be quicker.

3 (4-oz.) cans whole green
chilies
1/2 pound Monterey Jack
cheese, grated
1/2 pound sharp cheddar
cheese, grated

2. Split open chilies, remove seeds and drain on paper towels. Mix cheeses. Reserve 1/2 cup of cheese for topping.

1/2 cup canned tomato sauce

3. Make 2 alternate layers of remaining cheese, chilies and egg mixture in a deep 1½-quart casserole. Pour tomato sauce over top and sprinkle with reserved cheese. Cover with a paper towel. Hold towel in place with a wooden pick through center making sure towel does not touch cheese. (This helps absorb some of the moisture.) Microwave on **HIGH (100%) 10 MINUTES**. Rotate dish every two minutes.

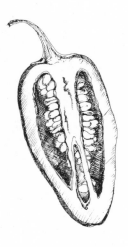

MEXICAN TORTILLA PIE

huevos con tortilla a la mexicana

With avocado slices

Cooking Time: 12 minutes
Utensil: 2-quart round glass casserole dish
Servings: 6

6 small flour tortillas

1. Line a buttered 2-quart round dish with 6 tortillas. Extend tops of tortillas to rim of dish.

1 (4-oz.) can whole green chilies, drained and seeded
1 large tomato, chopped
1/2 medium onion, thinly sliced

2. Place green chilies, tomato, and onion in bottom of dish on tortillas.

3 eggs, beaten
3 Tablespoons flour
1 teaspoon salt
1/2 teaspoon baking powder
1/2 cup milk
1 cup cheddar cheese, grated

3. In a mixing bowl, beat eggs and mix with flour, salt, baking powder and milk. Fold in cheese. Pour mixture over ingredients in the 2-quart dish. Microwave on **HIGH (100%) 12 MINUTES**.

Place avocado slices on top of pie and cut into wedges. Spoon mild taco sauce with each serving.

FRENCH ONION QUICHE

quiche aux oignons

Cooking Time: 24 minutes
Utensils: 10-inch ceramic quiche dish
2-quart glass dish
Servings: 8

1 (10-inch) pastry for quiche, baked

1. Follow directions on page 202 for Quiche Pastry.

2 pounds onions, cut in half through root end, thinly sliced
2 Tablespoons margarine
1 teaspoon salt

2. In a 2-quart dish, cook onions and margarine covered on **HIGH (100%) 15 MINUTES**. Stir one time. Stir in salt after cooking. Drain well in colander.

3 eggs
1/2 teaspoon salt
1/2 cup half and half cream
1/2 cup sour cream
1/2 teaspoon white pepper
1/4 teaspoon sage
Pinch each of ginger, ground cloves, nutmeg
1 cup Swiss cheese, shredded

3. Whisk eggs, salt, half and half, sour cream, white pepper, sage, ginger, cloves and nutmeg in a medium bowl until smooth. Stir in cheese. Spread well-drained onions evenly in baked pastry-lined quiche dish; pour egg mixture over onions. Microwave on **HIGH (100%) 8–9 MINUTES**. Let stand 10 minutes before serving.

SALMON QUICHE

quiche au saumon fumé

Cooking Time: 10 minutes
Utensils: 9-inch ceramic quiche dish
Servings: 6–8

1 (9-inch) quiche pastry, baked

1. Follow directions for quiche pastry on page 202.

1 (15½-oz.) can salmon, drained and boned
1/2 cup ripe olives, sliced
2 Tablespoons parsley, chopped
2 Tablespoons onion, chopped
1 cup Cheddar cheese, shredded

2. Flake salmon with a fork and add olives, parsley and onion. Spread evenly in baked pastry shell. Sprinkle cheese on top.

1 (13-oz.) can evaporated milk, undiluted
3 eggs, beaten
1/4 teaspoon salt
1/4 teaspoon garlic powder
1/4 teaspoon dry mustard
2 dashes Tabasco sauce

3. Combine milk, eggs, salt, garlic powder, dry mustard and Tabasco. Pour over salmon mixture. Microwave on **HIGH (100%) 10 MINUTES**, rotating dish at 3-minute intervals.

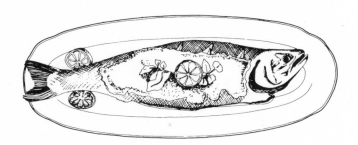

TOMATO QUICHE
quiche aux tomates

Cooking Time: 21 minutes 30 seconds
Utensils: 9 or 10-inch ceramic or glass quiche dish
4-cup glass measuring cup
Servings: 8

9 or 10-inch pastry for quiche, baked

1. Follow directions for Quiche Crust on page 202.

3 Tablespoons margarine
1 cup onion, finely chopped
3 large tomatoes, peeled, seeded, chopped and drained on paper towel
1 teaspoon salt
1/4 teaspoon thyme

2. Micromelt margarine in a 4-cup measure on **HIGH (100%) 30 SECONDS**. Add onions, tomatoes, salt and thyme. Sauté on **HIGH (100%) 7 MINUTES**. Cover with a paper towel to help reduce moisture.

6 slices bacon
1/2 pound Swiss cheese, coarsely grated or diced

3. Microwave bacon covered on a rack on **HIGH (100%) 5 MINUTES** until crisp. Crumble. Place cheese on bottom of cooked crust then bacon. Pour tomato mixture over cheese and bacon.

3 eggs, well beaten
3/4 cup half and half cream

4. Mix eggs and cream and pour over tomato mixture. Microwave on **HIGH (100%) 9 MINUTES**, rotating dish at 2-minute intervals. Center will still wiggle, but will finish cooking while standing 10 minutes. Slice in wedges and serve warm.

CINNAMON COFFEE CAKE

torta de canela

Cooking Time: 16 minutes 10 seconds
Utensils: 2-quart glass mixing bowl
　　　　　7 x 11-inch glass baking dish
Servings: 15

1/2 cup margarine, softened
1 cup brown sugar, packed
1 cup white sugar
2 cups all-purpose flour,
　unsifted
1½ teaspoons cinnamon
1 cup pecans, chopped

1 cup buttermilk
1/2 teaspoon baking soda
1/2 teaspoon baking powder
2 eggs, beaten
1 teaspoon vanilla extract

1. In a 2-quart glass mixing bowl, soften margarine on **HIGH (100%) 10 SECONDS**. Blend in sugars. Stir in flour and cinnamon until mixture is crumbly. For crumb topping, remove 1 cup of mixture and add pecans. Set aside.

2. To remaining mixture add buttermilk, baking soda, baking powder, eggs and vanilla. Beat until smooth. Pour batter into buttered 7 x 11-inch baking dish. Sprinkle with reserved crumb topping. Microwave on **MEDIUM (50%) 10 MINUTES**, rotating dish once. Then, microwave on **HIGH (100%) 6 MINUTES**, rotating dish once. Insert a wooden pick to test cake for doneness.

MICRO MEMO:

If brown sugar has become too hard to measure, place package of sugar (remove twist tie) in microwave on **HIGH (100%) 20–30 SECONDS**.

141

DATE BRAN MUFFINS

Cooking Time: 2–3 minutes per 6 muffins
Utensils: 6-cup micromuffin pan with paper liners
Servings: 4-dozen muffins

1 cup boiling water
3 cups 100% bran cereal,
    divided
1/2 cup margarine
1¼ cups sugar
2 eggs, beaten

2½ cups all-purpose flour
2 teaspoons soda
1/2 teaspoon salt
2 cups buttermilk
1/2 pound dates, chopped
1/2 cup pecans, chopped

1. Pour water over 1-cup bran cereal to soften. In a large bowl cream margarine, sugar, eggs and softened bran cereal.

2. Sift flour, soda and salt. Mix into creamed bran mixture, alternating with buttermilk. Add remaining 2 cups bran cereal, dates and nuts.

3. Using a microwave muffin pan with paper liners, fill half-full with batter. Microwave 6 muffins at a time on **HIGH (100%) 2–3 MINUTES**, rotating dish after 1 minute. Repeat using all the batter. Muffins freeze well, just reheat on **HIGH (100%) 10–20 SECONDS**. Ann Steiner and CiCi Williamson developed this recipe and they suggest keeping batter in the refrigerator up to 4 weeks and making fresh muffins for a quick breakfast.

LEMON BREAD
pain de citron

With *lemon syrup*

Cooking Time: 10 minutes
Utensils: 5 x 9-inch glass loaf dish
Servings: Makes 1 loaf

1/2 cup margarine
1 cup sugar
2 eggs
1/4 teaspoon salt
1/4 teaspoon soda
1½ cups all-purpose flour
1/2 cup buttermilk
1 teaspoon lemon rind,
   grated
2 Tablespoons lemon juice
1/2 cup pecans, chopped

LEMON SYRUP I:

Combine in 1-cup measure:
1/4 cup light corn syrup
2 Tablespoons lemon juice

LEMON SYRUP II:

Combine in 1-cup measure:
1/3 cup sugar
3 Tablespoons lemon juice

1. In a mixing bowl beat margarine and sugar together until creamy. Add eggs one at a time and blend. Sift together salt, soda and flour. Add to creamy mixture alternately with buttermilk. Fold in grated lemon rind, lemon juice and pecans. Line bottom of 5 x 9-inch loaf dish with wax paper. Pour batter into dish. Shield ends of loaf with foil.* Raise loaf dish in oven by placing on an inverted saucer or portable turntable. Microwave on **MEDIUM (50%) 7 MINUTES**, rotating dish 2 times. Remove foil strips and microwave on **HIGH (100%) 2–3 MINUTES**. Check for doneness by looking through bottom of dish. No unbaked batter should appear in center. Let stand 5 minutes before removing from dish. While bread is baking prepare Lemon Syrup I or II, both are delicious. Pour over warm loaf.

MICRO MEMO:

   For more even cooking in a 5 x 9-inch loaf dish, shield both ends of loaf with 2-inch wide strips of smooth foil. (Check your microwave manual on use of foil.) Foil should not touch sides of the microwave walls. Remove foil during the last 2 minutes of cooking.

BREAD

MEXICAN CORN BREAD

pan de maíz mexicano

Cooking Time: 17 minutes
Utensils: 8-cup glass measuring cup
9-inch round glass cake dish or large glass ring mold
Servings: 6

1/2 pound bacon, diced
3/4 cup yellow corn meal
1 egg
3/4 cup buttermilk
3/4 teaspoon baking soda
3/4 teaspoon salt
1 teaspoon garlic powder
1/4 cup bacon fat

1. Microwave diced bacon covered in an 8-cup measure on **HIGH (100%) 5 MINUTES**. Pour off fat (reserve 1/4 cup) and continue cooking on **HIGH (100%) 1 or 2 MINUTES** until bacon is crisp. Remove bacon and remaining fat. Drain, crumble and set aside. In the same dish mix together corn meal, egg, buttermilk, soda, salt, garlic powder and bacon fat. Mix well.

1 (8¾-oz.) can cream style corn
1 cup onion, chopped
3 jalapeño peppers, seeded and chopped
1½ cups Longhorn cheese, grated (any mild yellow cheese)

2. Stir in corn, onion, peppers, cheese and crumbled bacon. Pour into a greased 9-inch round dish. Microwave on **HIGH (100%) 10 MINUTES**. Rotate dish 3 times. Slice and serve warm.

PUMPKIN BREAD

pain de citrouille

Baked in a 2-cup measuring cup!

Cooking Time: 7 minutes per loaf
Utensil: 2-cup glass measuring cup
Servings: 5 loaves

3 cups sugar
1 cup vegetable oil
4 eggs, beaten
2/3 cup water
3½ cups all-purpose flour
1½ teaspoons salt
2 teaspoons baking soda
1 teaspoon nutmeg
1 teaspoon allspice
1 teaspoon cinnamon
1 teaspoon vanilla
1 (16-oz.) can pumpkin, solid
    pack
1 cup pecans, chopped

1. Combine sugar and oil in a large mixing bowl. Stir in eggs and mix well. Add water and flour, slowly. Add salt, baking soda, nutmeg, allspice, cinnamon, vanilla, pumpkin and pecans. Mix until blended. Line bottom of a 2-cup Pyrex measuring cup with a circle of wax paper (cut 5 or 6 circles for additional loaves). Pour 1⅓ cup batter in a 2-cup measure. Cover with vented plastic wrap. Microwave on **MEDIUM (50%) 7 MINUTES**, rotating cup 1/2 turn after 3 minutes.

2. Bread is done when no unbaked batter appears on sides of cup and center springs back when touched lightly. Cool uncovered 5 minutes. Remove from cup. Microwave 4 or 5 more loaves with remaining batter, using same measurements and timing. Serve warm. To reheat, place slices on plate. Cover loosely with plastic wrap. Microwave on **HIGH (100%) 30 SECONDS**. Loaves freeze well.

ONION BREAD

pain d'oignon

Cooking Time: Rising 40–60 minutes
              Bread 10 minutes 30 seconds
Utensils: 4-cup glass measuring cup
          1½-quart round glass casserole dish
Servings: Makes 1 loaf

1 (1⅜-oz.) package dry onion soup mix
1½ cups water
2 Tablespoons Parmesan cheese
1 Tablespoon sugar
1 Tablespoon vegetable oil

1. Combine onion soup mix and water in a 4-cup glass measure. Microwave on **HIGH (100%) 5 MINUTES**, stirring occasionally. Cool to lukewarm. Add cheese, sugar and oil.

1 (1/4-oz.) package active dry yeast
3 to 3½ cups all-purpose flour

2. Combine yeast with 1 cup flour in a large mixing bowl or large food processor bowl with steel blade. Add soup mixture and blend thoroughly. Mix in enough of the remaining flour to make a moderately stiff dough. Knead dough several minutes on a floured surface. Place dough in a lightly greased 1½-quart round casserole dish, turning dough once to grease surface. Cover with plastic wrap. Let rise until double in bulk, using shortcut rising method on page 147.

(Continued on next page)

ONION BREAD (Continued)

Corn meal
1/2 teaspoon bottled
    browning sauce
2 teaspoons water

3. After first rising, punch dough down and lift dough from dish. Sprinkle dish with corn meal and then return dough to dish. Brush top with a mixture of browning sauce and water. Cover with plastic wrap and continue to follow instructions in step 4, page 147. After the dough has risen the second time, uncover and remove container of water. Microwave on **HIGH (100%) 5 MINUTES 30 SECONDS**, rotating dish 2 times. Cool 5 minutes. Remove from dish, place on rack and allow to cool completely before slicing.

Onion bread is delicious toasted and buttered for breakfast.

SHORTCUT RISING METHOD
For yeast bread

1. Bring 3½ cups of water to a rolling boil in a 4-cup glass measure on **HIGH (100%) 7–8 MINUTES**. Place glass dish containing dough in microwave oven alongside container of boiling water. Microwave on **WARM (10%) 5 MINUTES** or **DEFROST 2 MINUTES**.

2. Let dough rise 20 to 30 minutes until doubled in bulk in a warm place.

3. Punch down dough. Form into desired shape according to bread recipe and place in prepared baking dish.

4. Again, bring 3½ cups of water to a boil in a 4-cup glass measure. Repeat steps 1 and 2 until dough doubles in bulk.

5. The dough is now ready for baking. Remove the container of water from oven and microwave as recipe directs.

MICRO MEMO:

    Ann Steiner and CiCi Williamson have developed this method to speed up rising of yeast breads using microwaves.

Vegetables
Salads

Vegetables:

legumbres   Spanish
legumi   Italian
legumes   French

In the microwave, vegetables retain their natural color, true flavor and valuable nutrients—crisp, tender or soft.

Salads:

ASPARAGUS SPEARS

asparagi

With lemon horseradish sauce

Cooking Time: Asparagus 14 minutes
 Sauce 4 minutes
Utensils: Round glass dish
 2-cup glass measuring cup
Servings: 6 (about 1½ cups sauce)

2 pounds fresh asparagus spears or 2 (10-oz.) cartons frozen asparagus spears

Trim tough portion at bottom of each asparagus spear. Rinse thoroughly, but do not dry. Arrange spears in a round dish with tips toward center and spear ends toward the outside. Cover with a tight-fitting lid or plastic wrap and microwave on **HIGH (100%) 7 MINUTES PER POUND**. If using frozen asparagus, remove outer waxed wrapper and place cartons on a plate. Microwave on **HIGH (100%) 7 MINUTES PER CARTON**.

LEMON HORSERADISH SAUCE:

1/4 cup margarine
2 Tablespoons onion, finely chopped
3 Tablespoons flour
1/2 teaspoon salt
3/4 cup water
Grated peel and juice of 1/2 lemon
3 teaspoons prepared horseradish
1 hard-cooked egg, chopped coarsely

Melt margarine in a 2-cup measure on **HIGH (100%) 1 MINUTE**. Add onion and microwave on **HIGH (100%) 1 MINUTE**. Stir in flour and salt. Gradually blend in water. Microwave on **HIGH (100%) 1 MINUTE 30 SECONDS**, stirring at 30-second intervals, until thickened. Add lemon juice, lemon peel, horseradish and chopped egg. Microwave on **HIGH (100%) 30 SECONDS**. Serve warm over cooked asparagus.

4TH OF JULY BAKED BEANS

—or any time of the year

Cooking Time: 30 minutes
Utensils: 7 x 11-inch glass baking dish
Servings: 6

8 slices bacon, diced
2/3 cup onion, chopped
2/3 cup green bell pepper,
** chopped**
1 clove garlic, chopped

2 (16-oz.) cans pork and
** beans**
1/3 cup brown sugar
3 Tablespoons dry mustard
1/4 cup Worcestershire sauce
1 teaspoon Creole seasoning
** OR 1 teaspoon mixture**
** of salt, black and red**
** pepper**

1. Place bacon, onion, bell pepper and garlic in a 7 x 11-inch baking dish. Cover with wax paper. Microwave on **HIGH (100%) 5 MINUTES**.

2. Stir in beans, brown sugar, mustard, Worcestershire sauce and Creole seasoning. Cover with wax paper. Microwave on **HIGH (100%) 20 MINUTES**, stirring at 10 minutes. Continue to microwave on **HIGH (100%) 5 MINUTES**, stirring at 2 minutes. Let stand covered 5 minutes before serving.

RANCH PINTO BEANS

frijoles ranchero

Pronounced free-HOH-lehs ran-chair-roh

Cooking Time: Soaking 1 hour 20 minutes
Beans 1 hour 5 minutes
Utensils: 4 or 5-quart ceramic casserole
Servings: 8–10

1 pound (2 cups) dry pinto beans
8 cups water
1/4 teaspoon baking soda

1. Wash beans and soak overnight in 8 cups water and soda or bring beans, soda and water to a boil on **HIGH (100%)** (approximately) **20 MINUTES**. Let sit covered 1 hour. Do not discard water.

1 large onion, cut in chunks
2 Tablespoons vegetable oil
1 Tablespoon chili powder

2. After soaking beans add onion, oil and chili powder. Cover and microwave on **HIGH (100%) 20 MINUTES**. Stir once.

2 cups smoked ham, cut in chunks
1 (10-oz.) can Ro-tel chilies and tomatoes, chopped with liquid
1 Tablespoon Hickory Smoked salt

3. Add ham. Cover and microwave on **MEDIUM (50%) 25 MINUTES**. Add Ro-tel chilies and tomatoes and salt. Cover and continue to microwave on **MEDIUM (50%) 20 MINUTES** or until beans are soft. Cook this dish early and reheat before serving, as this enhances the flavor of the beans.

Frijoles may be served as a side dish with Mexican food or over rice with corn bread.

RED BEANS À LA LOUISIANE

Cooking Time: 65 minutes plus soaking time
Utensil: 5-quart ceramic casserole
Servings: 8–10

1 pound red beans, soaked
1/2 teaspoon baking soda
8 cups water
1 cup onion, coarsely
    chopped
1/2 cup celery, chopped
1 clove garlic, minced
2 bay leaves
1/4 teaspoon basil
1/4 teaspoon thyme
1/4 teaspoon black pepper
1/4 teaspoon cayenne pepper
1/8 teaspoon Creole
    seasoning
1 small ham bone with meat

1/2 pound smoked sausage,
    sliced in rounds
1/2 pound ham, diced
1 Tablespoon salt or to taste

1. Wash beans and place in a 5-quart casserole with soda and water. Let beans soak overnight or using a quicker method, cover and microwave on **HIGH (100%)** (approximately) **20 MINUTES** until boiling. Continue boiling 2 minutes. Let stand on counter to soak 1 hour. Do not discard water. After soaking add onion, celery, garlic, bay leaves, basil, thyme, pepper, Creole seasoning and ham bone. Cover and microwave on **HIGH (100%) 20 MINUTES**.

2. Stir in sausage and ham. Cover and microwave on **MEDIUM (50%) 45 MINUTES** until beans are soft, stirring twice. Add salt during last 20 minutes of cooking. Serve the tender beans over a mound of rice.

SNAPPY GREEN BEANS

haricots verts croquants

With mustard sauce

Cooking Time: 9 minutes 30 seconds
Utensils: 1½-quart glass casserole
          4-cup glass measuring cup
Servings: 6

2 (16-oz.) cans whole green beans, drained reserving 1 cup liquid for sauce

1. Place 1 can of drained beans in a lightly greased 1½-quart casserole dish.

4 Tablespoons margarine
4 Tablespoons flour
1 Tablespoon dry mustard
1 teaspoon salt
1/4 teaspoon white pepper
1 cup Cheddar cheese, grated

2. Prepare mustard sauce. Micromelt margarine in a 4-cup measure on **HIGH (100%) 1 MINUTE**. Stir in flour and dry mustard. Add 1 cup of bean liquid. Microwave on **HIGH (100%) 1 MINUTE 30 SECONDS**, stirring at 30 second intervals until thickened. Add salt, pepper and grated cheese.

1/3 cup seasoned bread crumbs mixed with
1 Tablespoon melted margarine

3. Pour half the sauce over beans. Repeat layers, spreading second can of drained beans then remaining sauce. Top with buttered bread crumbs. Microwave on **HIGH (100%) 7 MINUTES** until heated through.

MICRO MEMO:

*To make quick buttered bread crumbs, place margarine or butter on top of crumbs in a glass measuring cup. Microwave on **HIGH (100%)** just until butter melts. Stir to mix.*

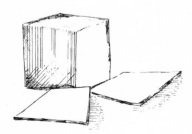

PROSCIUTTO BROCCOLI MOUSSE

With sautéed cherry tomatoes

Cooking Time: 36 minutes
Utensils: Microsafe plate
 6 or 8-cup glass ring mold
Servings: 10

4 (10-oz.) packages frozen chopped broccoli
1 teaspoon salt
1/2 cup Parmesan cheese, freshly grated
1 cup onion, chopped
1 clove garlic, minced
1 teaspoon salt
1 teaspoon freshly ground pepper
1/8 teaspoon freshly grated nutmeg

1. After removing outer waxed wrappers, place cartons of broccoli on a plate. Microwave 2 cartons at a time on **HIGH (100%) 14 MINUTES**, or a total of 28 minutes for the 4 cartons. Sprinkle salt on after cooking. Drain broccoli in a colander and press out excess liquid on paper towels. Purée in food processor or blender and transfer to a 3-quart mixing bowl. Add Parmesan cheese, onion, garlic, salt, pepper and nutmeg.

1/4 pound prosciutto ham, sliced paper thin

2. Line a lightly oiled 6 or 8-cup glass ring mold with prosciutto ham slices letting ham overhang inner and outer rims. It will be overlapped after filling has been added.

4 eggs
3/4 cup evaporated milk, undiluted

3. In a small bowl, beat eggs and evaporated milk and fold into broccoli mixture until well blended. Pour into mold and fold prosciutto ham over broccoli mixture. Cover mold with a paper towel and microwave on **HIGH (100%) 8 MINUTES**, rotating dish at 2-minute intervals. Unmold by running a thin knife around mold. Serve hot centered with a garnish of sautéed cherry tomatoes. See recipe on page 171.

CARROTS AU GRATIN

carote con formaggio grattugiato

Cooking Time: 30 minutes
Utensils: 9-inch round glass dish
      4-cup glass measuring cup
      7 x 11-inch glass baking dish
Servings: 8

**2 pounds carrots, sliced
   round
2 Tablespoons butter**

1. Place carrots in a 9-inch dish. Dot with butter (no water or salt), cover tightly with thin plastic wrap and microwave on **HIGH (100%) 12 MINUTES** until tender. Stir or shake dish after 5 minutes. Set aside covered.

**1/4 cup butter
1 cup onion, minced
1/4 cup flour
1 teaspoon dry mustard
1 teaspoon snipped parsley
2 cups milk
1 teaspoon salt
1/4 teaspoon celery salt
1/8 teaspoon white pepper**

2. In a 4-cup measure melt butter and add onions. Sauté on **HIGH (100%) 3 MINUTES**. Stir in flour, mustard and parsley. Slowly stir in milk. Microwave on **HIGH (100%) 9 MINUTES**, stirring at 3-minute intervals until thickened. Add salt, celery salt and pepper.

**6 ounces processed American
   cheese slices
1½ cups buttered or
   seasoned bread crumbs**

3. Place half of the cooked carrots in a flat baking dish. Cover with cheese slices and top with remaining carrots. Pour white sauce over carrots. Sprinkle on bread crumbs. Microwave on **HIGH (100%) 6 MINUTES** turning dish once.

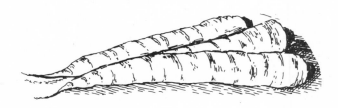

PAT'S CARROTS AND BANANAS

Taste is similar to Bananas Foster

Cooking Time: 13 minutes
Utensils: 2-quart glass dish
            2-cup glass measuring cup
Servings: 6–8

1 pound fresh carrots, peeled and cut in 1-inch diagonal slices
1/4 cup water

1. Microwave carrots with water in a 2-quart dish covered on **HIGH (100%) 8 MINUTES** until tender. Drain.

1/4 cup margarine
1 Tablespoon cinnamon
1/4 cup brown sugar

2. In a 2-cup measure melt margarine on **HIGH (100%) 1 MINUTE**. Add cinnamon and sugar and pour over carrots. Cover. Microwave on **HIGH (100%) 1 MINUTE**.

4 bananas, peeled and cut in 1-inch diagonal slices

3. Stir bananas into mixture. Cover and microwave on **HIGH (100%) 3 MINUTES**.

STUFFED CAULIFLOWER

cavolfiori ripieni alla bechamelle

Cooking Time: 19 minutes 30 seconds
Utensils: Paper plate
2 (4-cup) glass measuring cups
Round glass serving dish
Servings: 6

1½ pound cauliflower, whole
1/4 teaspoon salt

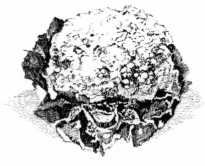

1. Rinse cauliflower. Place on a paper plate and wrap cauliflower and plate with plastic wrap. Microwave on **HIGH (100%) 3 MINUTES**. Turn cauliflower over and microwave on **HIGH (100%) 4 MINUTES 30 SECONDS** or until stems are tender. Sprinkle salt on after cooking. Scoop out top center (about 1 cup) of cauliflower and chop pieces finely. Place scooped-out cauliflower in a serving dish covered with plastic wrap to keep warm.

2 eggs, hard-cooked

2. Hard boil eggs conventionally, chop and set aside.

2 Tablespoons margarine
1 cup onion, chopped
1/3 cup bell pepper, chopped
1 rib celery, chopped

3. Micromelt margarine in a 4-cup measure on **HIGH (100%) 30 SECONDS**. Add onion, bell pepper, celery and the 1 cup of chopped cauliflower. Sauté on **HIGH (100%) 3 MINUTES**.

2 Tablespoons margarine
2 Tablespoons flour
1/8 teaspoon white pepper
1/4 teaspoon salt
1 cup milk
1/4 cup parsley, minced
Seasoned bread crumbs
1 Tablespoon margarine

4. Melt margarine in a 4-cup measure on **HIGH (100%) 30 SECONDS**. Stir in flour, pepper and salt until smooth. Add milk stirring to blend. Microwave on **HIGH (100%) 4 MINUTES**, stirring every minute until thickened. Add parsley, chopped eggs and sautéed vegetables. Pour over scooped out cauliflower. Sprinkle on bread crumbs and dot with margarine. Microwave on **HIGH (100%) 4 MINUTES**.

GREEN CHILIES AND CORN

chiles verdes y maíz

Cooking Time: 16 minutes
Utensils: 2-quart glass mixing bowl
         7 x 11-inch glass baking dish
Servings: 6

1/2 cup margarine
1 (4-oz.) can whole green
   chilies, seeded and
   chopped
1/2 cup yellow corn meal
2 eggs, beaten
1 cup dairy sour cream
1 teaspoon salt
1/2 pound Monterey Jack
   cheese, grated
1/2 pound Cheddar cheese,
   grated
1 (16-oz.) can whole kernel
   corn, drained (reserve 2
   tablespoons liquid)

Micromelt margarine in a 2-quart mixing bowl on **HIGH (100%) 1 MINUTE.** Add green chilies, corn meal, eggs, sour cream, salt, cheese and corn which has been chopped with 2 tablespoons of corn liquid in food processor. Mix thoroughly. Pour into buttered 7 x 11-inch baking dish. Microwave on **MEDIUM-HIGH (70%) 10 MINUTES.** Stir mixture at 2 minute intervals. Finish cooking on **HIGH (100%) 5 MINUTES** until firm.

SHOE PEG CORN CASSEROLE

casserole de maïs shoe peg

Cooking Time: 13 minutes
Utensils: 2-cup glass measuring cup
        1½-quart glass casserole
Servings: 4–6

2 Tablespoons butter
1/2 cup onion, chopped

1. In a 2-cup measure melt butter on **HIGH (100%) 1 MINUTE** and add onion. Cover with wax paper and microwave on **HIGH (100%) 2 MINUTES** or until onion is tender.

1 (10-oz.) can Ro-Tel
    tomatoes and chilies
1/2 Tablespoon dry onion
    soup mix

2. With a slotted spoon remove tomatoes and crush with a fork. Add tomatoes and soup mix to onions. Stir to mix well. Cover and microwave on **HIGH (100%) 2 MINUTES**.

1 (12-oz.) can Shoe Peg
    whole kernel white
    corn, drained
1 (8½-oz.) can cream style
    corn

3. Place tomato mixture and corn in a 1½-quart casserole. Mix well, cover, and microwave on **HIGH (100%) 8 MINUTES**. Stir one time.

EGGPLANT ELEGANTE

melanzane elegante

Cooking Time: 26 minutes 30 seconds
Utensils: 3-quart glass or ceramic casserole
4-cup glass measuring cup
Servings: 6–8

**2 medium eggplants, peeled
and diced
1 teaspoon margarine
1 Tablespoon seasoned salt
1 Tablespoon flour**

1. Place eggplant in a 3-quart casserole. Dot margarine on top and cover with plastic wrap or a tight lid. Microwave on **HIGH (100%) 10 MINUTES**. Drain well and sprinkle with seasoned salt and flour. Mix gently. Set aside covered.

**1 Tablespoon margarine
1 Tablespoon olive oil
1 cup onion, diced
1/2 cup green bell pepper,
diced
1 clove garlic, minced**

2. Heat margarine and oil in a 4-cup measure on **HIGH (100%) 30 SECONDS**. Add onion, bell pepper and garlic and sauté on **HIGH (100%) 4 MINUTES** until soft.

**1/4 pound fresh mushrooms,
thinly sliced
1 (16-oz.) can tomatoes,
drained and chopped or
3 large tomatoes,
peeled, seeded and
diced
1 Tablespoon parsley,
chopped
1 teaspoon salt
1/4 teaspoon pepper
1/2 teaspoon thyme
1/4 cup freshly grated
Parmesan cheese**

3. Add mushrooms, tomatoes, parsley, salt, pepper and thyme. Microwave on **HIGH (100%) 3 MINUTES**. Pour tomato mixture over drained eggplant. Mix. Top with Parmesan cheese. Microwave on **HIGH (100%) 9 MINUTES**.

EGGPLANT MOUSSAKA

aubergine moussaka

Cooking Time: 19 minutes
Utensils: Shallow 2-quart glass dish
Plastic colander and glass bowl
1½-quart glass casserole
Servings: 4–6

**1 (1-lb.) eggplant, peeled and
cut into 1/2-inch cubes
2 teaspoons butter
1/4 teaspoon salt**

1. Microwave eggplant and butter in a shallow dish covered with plastic wrap on **HIGH (100%) 5 MINUTES**. Drain, sprinkle lightly with salt and set aside covered.

**1 pound lean ground beef
1/3 cup onion, chopped
1 garlic clove, minced
1/2 teaspoon salt
1/4 teaspoon pepper**

2. Crumble meat loosely in a plastic colander over a bowl (to catch drippings). Cover with wax paper. Microwave on **HIGH (100%) 2 MIN-UTES**. Stir well and sprinkle onions and garlic on top. Cover and con-tinue to microwave on **HIGH (100%) 3 MINUTES**. Add salt and pepper after cooking. Cover while preparing Béchamel Sauce*.

**3/4 cup Parmesan cheese,
grated**

3. Place a layer of eggplant in the bottom of a 1½-quart dish. Place all of the meat on top. Add another layer of eggplant. Pour Béchamel Sauce over and sprinkle 3/4 cup grated Parmesan cheese on top. Microwave on **HIGH (100%) 4 MINUTES**.

*BÉCHAMEL SAUCE:
Makes 1 cup

**2 Tablespoons butter
2 Tablespoons flour
1 Tablespoon onion, finely
chopped
1 cup chicken bouillon
2 teaspoons heavy cream
1/4 teaspoon salt
Dash white pepper**

In a 2-cup measure melt butter on **HIGH (100%) 1 MINUTE**. Stir in flour and onions and microwave on **HIGH (100%) 1 MINUTE**. Add bouillon and cream slowly. Microwave on **HIGH (100%) 3 MINUTES**, stirring every 30 seconds. Add salt and pepper.

SCALLOPED EGGPLANT

melanzane al gratino

Cooking Time: 15 minutes
Utensils: 2-quart glass dish
2-cup glass measuring cup
Servings: 6

1 large (1½-lb.) eggplant, peeled and diced into 1/2-inch cubes
1/3 cup onion, minced
1 teaspoon margarine

1/3 cup margarine
1¼ cups dry seasoned herb stuffing (Pepperidge Farm), divided

1 (10¾-oz.) can cream of mushroom soup, undiluted
1/3 cup milk
1 egg, slightly beaten
1 teaspoon salt
1/4 teaspoon white pepper
1/2 cup Cheddar cheese, grated

1. Place eggplant, onion and margarine in a 2-quart dish. Microwave covered on **HIGH (100%) 8 MINUTES**. Stir once. Drain.

2. Micromelt margarine over herb stuffing in a 2-cup measure on **HIGH (100%) 1 MINUTE**. Stir to mix. Reserve 1/4 cup for topping.

3. Add herb stuffing, mushroom soup, milk, egg, salt and pepper to the eggplant. Mix thoroughly. Top with 1/4 cup reserved herb stuffing and cheese. Microwave on **HIGH (100%) 6 MINUTES**. Rotate dish once or twice.

STUFFED ONIONS

oignons farcis

Cooking Time: 35 minutes
Utensils: 7 x 11-inch glass baking dish
Plastic colander and glass mixing bowl
2-cup glass measuring cup
Servings: 10

10 medium onions
2 Tablespoons butter

1 pound beef, ground round
1 clove garlic, minced
1/2 cup Mozzarella cheese,
shredded
2 teaspoons snipped parsley
1/4 teaspoon pepper
1 teaspoon Creole seasoning
or all-purpose seasoning
1 egg, beaten

1/2 cup beef broth soup,
undiluted
1/3 cup tomato sauce
1 bay leaf or a pinch of
laurier

1. Peel and slice off root end and top of onions. Place onions in a large flat dish. Dot tops with butter (do not add water or salt). Cover tightly with plastic wrap and microwave on **HIGH (100%) 25 MINUTES**. Rotate dish once. Drain and hollow each onion. Set aside covered in same dish.

2. Place meat and garlic in a plastic colander over a glass mixing bowl. Cover with wax paper and microwave on **HIGH (100%) 4 MINUTES**. Stir meat at 2 minutes so it will not lump. Discard meat drippings and return meat to mixing bowl. Add cheese, parsley, seasonings and egg. Divide mixture evenly among hollowed onions.

3. Mix beef broth, tomato sauce and bay leaf in a 2-cup measure. Microwave on **HIGH (100%) 1 MINUTE** and pour over stuffed onions. Cover with wax paper. Microwave on **HIGH (100%) 5 MINUTES** until heated through. Extra Mozzarella cheese may be sprinkled on after cooking.

MICRO MEMO:

To heat stuffed onions individually, allow 1 minute on **HIGH (100%)** *per onion.*

BLACK-EYED PEAS MEXICANA

chícaros mexicanos

Cooking Time: 33 minutes 30 seconds
Utensils: 1-quart glass bowl
        Plastic colander and pie plate
        2-quart glass casserole
Servings: 6

**1 (16 oz.) package frozen
   black-eyed peas
2 Tablespoons water
2 Tablespoons margarine
1 teaspoon salt
1/8 teaspoon red pepper**

1. In a 1-quart bowl add peas, water and margarine. Cover with plastic wrap and microwave on **HIGH (100%) 11 MINUTES**. Add salt and pepper. Cover and set aside.

**1 pound bulk pork sausage
1 cup onion, chopped
1 clove garlic, chopped**

2. In a plastic colander mix sausage, onion and garlic. Place colander in a pie plate, cover with wax paper and microwave on **HIGH (100%) 7 MINUTES 30 SECONDS**, stirring at 2 minute intervals.

**2 teaspoons chili powder
1/4 teaspoon pepper
1 (16-oz.) can tomatoes with
   liquid, chopped
1 jalapeño pepper, cut in 4
   strips (for milder flavor
   omit jalapeño pepper)**

3. Transfer sausage to a 2-quart casserole. Stir in chili powder and pepper. Add cooked black-eyed peas, tomatoes and 4 strips of jalapeño pepper. Cover and microwave on **HIGH (100%) 15 MINUTES**, stir 2 times.

165

CHEESE POTATOES

papas con queso

Cooking Time: 40 minutes
Utensils: 7 x 11-inch glass baking dish
4-cup glass measuring cup
Servings: 8–10

**2½–3 pounds potatoes
(6 cups cubed)
1 (4-oz.) jar pimientos,
drained and chopped**

**1/4 cup margarine
1 cup onion, chopped
1/4 cup flour
2 teaspoons salt
1/2 teaspoon dry mustard
1/2 teaspoon paprika
1/4 teaspoon white pepper
2 cups milk**

1. Peel potatoes and cut into large cubes. Toss potatoes and pimientos together in a greased 7 x 11-inch baking dish.

2. In a 4-cup measure melt margarine on **HIGH (100%) 1 MINUTE**. Add onion and sauté on **HIGH (100%) 3 MINUTES**. Stir in flour, salt, mustard, paprika and pepper. Blend well and slowly add milk to make a white sauce. Microwave on **HIGH (100%) 6 MINUTES** stirring every 2 minutes until thickened.

3. Stir sauce into potato mixture. Cover with plastic wrap. Microwave on **HIGH (100%) 20 MINUTES**. Stir and rearrange potatoes for even cooking at 10 minutes.

**1 pound American cheese,
cubed**

4. Stir cheese cubes into potatoes. Microwave uncovered on **HIGH (100%) 10 MINUTES**.

PARSLEY-BUTTERED NEW POTATOES

pommes de terre primeurs au beurre de persil

Cooking Time: 15 minutes
Utensils: 2-quart glass casserole
            1-cup glass measuring cup
Servings: 6

2 pounds new potatoes
1/4 cup water
1/4 cup margarine
2 Tablespoons snipped fresh
parsley
1/2 teaspoon lemon juice, or
more to taste

1. Wash potatoes and remove 1/2-inch peel around center of each potato with a small knife. Place potatoes and water in a 2-quart casserole, arranging them in a circle with smaller potatoes in the center. Cover tightly with plastic wrap or lid. Microwave on **HIGH (100%) 14 MINUTES**. Let sit covered 6 minutes. Place margarine, parsley and lemon juice in a 1-cup measure. Microwave on **HIGH (100%) 1 MINUTE** or until hot. Drain potatoes and pour sauce over them.

SWEET POTATO PUDDING

Grandmother's favorite

Cooking Time: 30 minutes
Utensil: 5-quart ceramic casserole
Servings: 8

2 pounds sweet potatoes,
peeled and grated
1/2 cup sugar
1 teaspoon salt
1 cup dark corn syrup
3 eggs, well beaten
1/2 cup butter or margarine,
softened
Grated rind of 1/2 orange

Grate sweet potatoes by hand or use steel blade of food processor. Quarter and process one yam at a time coarsely. Place in a large mixing bowl along with sugar and salt. Add corn syrup, eggs, margarine and grated orange rind. Mix well and pour into a greased 5-quart casserole. Microwave on **HIGH (100%) 30 MINUTES**; stir at 10 minute intervals. Let stand and cool until firm enough to slice. Serve plain or with whipped cream for a dessert.

RATATOUILLE

A summer garden feast pronounced ra ta tyū ē.

Cooking Time: 16 minutes
Utensil: 2 or 2½-quart glass casserole
Servings: 6

1 Tablespoon olive oil
2 medium onions, sliced into
   rings
2 cloves garlic, minced
1 pound eggplant, peeled
   and cubed
1 large green bell pepper,
   seeded, cut into strips
1 pound zucchini, sliced in
   sticks unpeeled

3 ripe firm tomatoes,
   peeled*, seeded, juiced
   and sliced into strips
2 teaspoons salt (more or
   less to taste)
1/2 teaspoon basil
1/2 teaspoon thyme
1/4 teaspoon red pepper

1. Sauté onions, garlic and olive oil in a 2 or 2½-quart covered casserole on **HIGH (100%) 4 MINUTES**. Add eggplant, green pepper and zucchini. Cover with paper towel. Cook on **HIGH (100%) 7 MINUTES**, stirring once.

2. Add tomatoes, and a mixture of salt, basil, thyme and red pepper. Mix lightly. Cover with paper towel and microwave on **HIGH (100%) 5 MINUTES** until vegetables are tender. Ratatouille can be served hot or cold.

MICRO MEMOS:

*To peel tomatoes quickly, place 3 firm tomatoes in a plastic bag and twist bag without tying. Microwave on **HIGH (100%) 3 MINUTES**.
To seed and juice tomatoes, cut peeled tomato crosswise (not through stem). Squeeze each half gently to extract seeds and juice from the center of the tomato.

BEBE'S JALAPEÑO SPINACH

espinaca con jalapeño a la bebe

Cooking Time: 10 minutes
Utensils: 2-quart glass dish
Servings: 6

2 Tablespoons margarine
1/2 cup onion, chopped
1 Tablespoon flour
3/4 cup drained liquid from 1
(15-oz.) can spinach

1. Micromelt margarine in a 2-quart dish on **HIGH (100%) 1 MINUTE**. Add onions and sauté on **HIGH (100%) 2 MINUTES**. Stir in flour and slowly add liquid from spinach. Microwave on **HIGH (100%) 5 MINUTES**, stirring at 2-minute intervals until thickened.

1 (8-oz.) jar Jalapeño pepper
Cheez Whiz
2 Tablespoons Worcestershire
sauce
1/2 teaspoon garlic powder

2. Stir in cheese until melted. Add Worcestershire sauce and garlic powder.

2 (15-oz.) cans spinach,
drained well and cut
with kitchen shears

3. Fold in drained spinach. Microwave on **HIGH (100%) 2 MINUTES** until heated through.

Goes well with game, beef and chicken.

Jalapeño Spinach is also delicious as a dip. Instead of cutting through the spinach with shears, give the spinach a quick whirl in the food processor before folding into cheese sauce. The color and texture will change.

Try using the "dip" over drained oysters in ramekins or shells as a quick Oysters Rockefeller.

SPINACH WITH GARLIC

spinace con aglio

Cooking Time: 10 minutes
Utensils: 3-quart glass casserole dish
Servings: 4

2 pounds fresh spinach
1/4 cup water

1. Clean spinach well. Discard all large stems and place dripping wet into a 3-quart dish. Add water to allow vegetable to steam in its own juices. Cover and microwave on **HIGH (100%) 4 MINUTES** until spinach wilts. Stir and continue to microwave on **HIGH (100%) 5 MINUTES**.

6 cloves garlic, minced
1/4 teaspoon salt
1/2 teaspoon pepper
1/4 cup olive oil

2. Mince garlic and throw into the dish with spinach. Add salt and pepper and dribble liberally with olive oil. Cover and steam on **HIGH (100%) 1–2 MINUTES** until flavors have had an opportunity to blend. Adjust seasoning and serve in small bowls with crusty bread to dip into juices.

One of the many favorite Italian recipes of the Guercio family.

CALICO SQUASH BAKE
calabaza calico al horno

Cooking Time: 18 minutes
Utensils: 2-quart glass casserole dish
Servings: 6

**4 pounds yellow squash,
   sliced
1/2 cup onions, finely
   chopped
1/4 cup margarine**

1. In a 2-quart dish microwave squash, onions and margarine covered on **HIGH (100%) 10 MINUTES**. Drain.

**1¼ cups seasoned bread
   crumbs
1 (4-oz.) jar pimientos, diced
1½ teaspoons salt
1/4 teaspoon white pepper
2 eggs, beaten**

2. Stir in bread crumbs, pimiento, salt and pepper. Add beaten eggs and toss lightly to mix. Microwave covered on **HIGH (100%) 8 MINUTES**.

CHERRY TOMATO SAUTÉ

pomodori fritti al burro

Cooking Time: 1 minute 30 seconds
Utensil: 1-quart glass casserole
Servings: 6

**1 pint box cherry tomatoes,
   about 22
2 Tablespoons margarine
1/4 teaspoon sugar
1/4 teaspoon salt
1/8 teaspoon freshly ground
   pepper
1 Tablespoon chopped
   parsley for garnish**

Remove stems, wash and dry cherry tomatoes. Melt margarine in a 1-quart casserole on **HIGH (100%) 30 SECONDS**. Add tomatoes and sprinkle with sugar. Microwave on **HIGH (100%) 1 MINUTE**. Season with salt and pepper and garnish with chopped parsley.

SQUASH MORELLE

calabaza morelle

An interesting and tasty dish for dinner parties.

Cooking Time: 24 minutes
Utensils: 2-quart glass or ceramic casserole
Servings: 6

2 pounds yellow squash, sliced
1 cup onions, chopped
1 teaspoon butter

1. Place squash and onions in a 2-quart casserole dish. Dot with butter and cover tightly with plastic wrap. Microwave on **HIGH (100%) 16 MINUTES**. Shake dish once or twice to rearrange contents. (Shaking eliminates removing the cover.) Drain and mash.

2 eggs, beaten
1/2 cup sour cream
2 Tablespoons butter, softened
1 Tablespoon sugar
1½ teaspoons salt
1/2 cup Mozzarella cheese

2. Mix together eggs, sour cream, butter, sugar, salt and cheese and stir into squash. Microwave on **HIGH (100%) 4 MINUTES**.

1/2 cup ground almonds

3. Sprinkle on ground almonds and microwave on **HIGH (100%) 4 MINUTES** more.

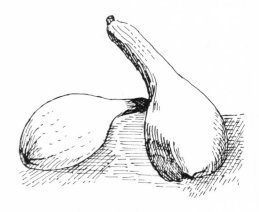

STUFFED TURNIPS

navets farcis

Cooking Time: 31 minutes
Utensils: 7 x 11-inch glass baking dish or
Large round dish
Flat 10-inch ceramic dish
Servings: 6

6 medium turnips (2½ to 3 pounds), peeled with bottom sliced off so turnip sits straight
1/4 cup water
1/2 teaspoon sugar

1. Place 6 turnips in a 7 x 11-inch baking dish. Pour sugared water over turnips and cover tightly with plastic wrap. Microwave on **HIGH (100%) 15 MINUTES**. Turn dish once. When cool, use a melon baller to core turnips leaving a 1/4-inch shell. Reserve cores. Drain dish, return turnips, cover and set aside.

4 slices bacon
1 pound lean pork, diced
1/2 pound fresh mushrooms, quartered (optional)

2. In a flat 10-inch dish microwave bacon covered until crisp on **HIGH (100%) 4 MINUTES**. Crumble and set aside. In remaining bacon fat sauté diced pork, turnip cores and mushrooms (optional) covered on **HIGH (100%) 6 MINUTES**. Stir once. Drain or remove mixture with slotted spoon to bowl.

2 teaspoons Creole seasoning (or your favorite)
1/2 teaspoon white pepper
1 (8½-oz.) can sweet peas, Petit Pois, drained
Seasoned bread crumbs for sprinkling

3. Add Creole seasoning, pepper and peas. Toss lightly and stuff into turnip shells. Return to 7 x 11-inch dish and top with crumbled bacon and bread crumbs. Microwave on **HIGH (100%) 6 MINUTES**.

173

VEGETABLE MEDLEY

pot-pourri aux légumes

Cooking Time: 12 minutes
Utensil: 12-inch round glass plate
Servings: 8

1/2 head cauliflower, cut into flowerets
1/2 bunch broccoli, cut into flowerets
1 (12-oz.) bag medium carrots, sliced round, diagonal or in sticks
1 yellow squash, sliced round
1 zucchini, sliced round or in sticks
2 medium onions, quartered or 4 miniature onions
6 whole Brussels sprouts
4 large whole mushrooms
1 green or red bell pepper, cut in rings

1. Arrange rinsed and prepared vegetables on a 12-inch glass plate in an attractive, colorful way with the harder vegetables, cauliflower, broccoli and carrots, on the outer edge of plate. Place the softer vegetables, squash and zucchini, in the center of plate with onions, Brussels sprouts and mushrooms midway between the outer and center circles. Place slices of bell pepper on top. Do not season or add water. Cover tightly with thin plastic wrap (will take two sheets). Do not puncture. Microwave on **HIGH (100%) 10 MINUTES**. Check vegetables for doneness (test carrots) remembering to lift wrap away from you. Cook an additional **2 MINUTES** for softer vegetables. Cooking time is approximately 5 minutes per pound of vegetables.

1/4 cup margarine, melted
1–2 teaspoons Morton Nature's Seasons or Jane's Krazy Mixed-Up salt

2. Drain liquid from vegetables, reserve for soup or gravy, and pour or squeeze margarine over cooked vegetables. Sprinkle with seasoned salt.

174

YAM COCONUT PEACH BAKE

casserole aux patates et coco et pêches

Try this for dessert, too.

Cooking Time: 11 minutes
Utensil: 1-quart glass baking dish
Servings: 8

**2 (16-oz.) cans Louisiana
    yams, drained
2 eggs
1/4 cup margarine, softened
1/2 cup brown sugar
3/4 teaspoon salt
1/4 teaspoon cinnamon
2 Tablespoons rum, (light or
    dark)**

1. Mash yams in a large bowl or food processor with steel blade. Add eggs, margarine, brown sugar, salt, cinnamon and rum. Beat or process until mixture is light and fluffy. Turn into greased 1-quart dish or large pie plate with high sides. Microwave on **HIGH (100%) 9 MINUTES**. Rotate dish at 2 minute intervals.

**2/3 cup shredded coconut
1/4 teaspoon cinnamon
2 medium fresh peaches,
    peeled, pitted and sliced**

2. Toss coconut with cinnamon. Sprinkle a border of coconut around edge of casserole. Arrange peach slices inside border. Microwave on **HIGH (100%) 2 MINUTES** to warm peaches.

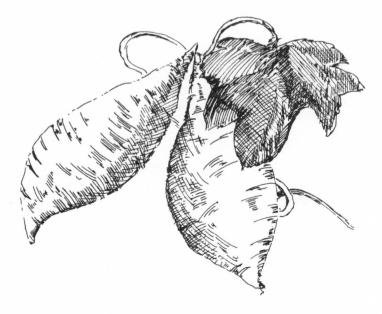

ZUCCHINI AU GRATIN

zucchini con formaggio grattugiato

Cooking Time: 15 minutes
Utensils: Bacon rack*
         1½-quart glass casserole
Servings: 6 to 8

3 slices bacon
1/4 cup seasoned bread
    crumbs

1. Cook bacon on a rack on **HIGH (100%) 2½ to 3 MINUTES**. Crumble, mix with bread crumbs and set aside.

4 cups zucchini, thinly sliced
1 teaspoon margarine

2. Place zucchini in a 1½-quart casserole. Dot with margarine and cover with plastic wrap tightly to steam. Microwave on **HIGH (100%) 7 MINUTES**. Drain.

1 egg
1/2 cup dairy sour cream
1 Tablespoon flour
3/4 cup sharp Cheddar
    cheese, shredded
1/2 teaspoon salt
1/4 teaspoon pepper

3. In a mixing bowl beat egg. Stir in sour cream, flour, cheese, salt, and pepper until blended. Stir into zucchini. Microwave on **HIGH (100%) 3 MINUTES**. Stir. Sprinkle bacon and bread crumbs over casserole. Microwave on **HIGH (100%) 2 MINUTES**.

*MICRO MEMO:

To make a disposable bacon rack, fold a sturdy paper plate in half and wedge it inside a 5 x 7-inch glass loaf dish. Drape the bacon over the paper plate, cover with wax paper and microwave on **HIGH (100%) 1 MINUTE** *per slice of bacon. All the grease drains in to the dish. Remove the bacon and throw away the paper plate. Reserve bacon fat and refrigerate.*

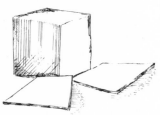

ZUCCHINI ITALIANO

zucchini all'italiano

Cooking Time: 12 minutes
Utensils: 10-inch square dish
Servings: 4

**1 large (or 2 small) onion,
  sliced in rings
4 Tablespoons olive oil
4 fresh tomatoes, peeled and
  cut into pieces or 2 cups
  canned, whole
  tomatoes, chopped**

**2½ pounds zucchini, (about 4
  cups) unpeeled, sliced in
  1/2-inch rounds
1 teaspoon salt or more
1/2 teaspoon pepper or more
1 bay leaf
1/2 teaspoon dried basil
  leaves or 1 to 2
  teaspoons fresh basil**

1. Place onions and oil in a 10-inch square dish. Cover. Microwave on **HIGH (100%) 3 MINUTES** until soft. Add chopped tomatoes, cover and microwave on **HIGH (100%) 3 MINUTES**.

2. Add zucchini, salt and pepper. Stir to mix. Microwave uncovered on **HIGH (100%) 4 MINUTES** until barely tender. Add bay leaf and basil leaves and microwave on **HIGH (100%) 2 MINUTES** longer.

BROCCOLI SALAD RING

insalata di broccoli

Cooking Time: 16 minutes
Utensils: Microwave-safe plate
        3-quart mixing bowl
        2-cup glass measuring cup
        1½-quart ring mold
Servings: 8–10

6 hard-cooked eggs, (not in microwave) shelled and chopped fine with steel blade in food processor
3/4 cup mayonnaise

1. Cook eggs conventionally in water to cover with 1/4 teaspoon salt (for easy peeling). Chop and place in a 3-quart mixing bowl. Add mayonnaise.

2 (10-oz.) packages frozen chopped broccoli
1/2 teaspoon salt

2. Remove outer waxed wrappers and place broccoli cartons on a plate. Microwave on **HIGH (100%) 14 MINUTES**. Drain, add salt and cool. Add to egg mixture.

1 envelope Knox unflavored gelatin (1 Tablespoon)
1 (10½-oz.) can beef consommé (gelatin added), undiluted

3. Soak gelatin in 1/4 cup cool consommé. In a 2-cup measure heat remaining consommé on **HIGH (100%) 1–2 MINUTES**. Add soaked gelatin to warm consommé and stir to dissolve. Cool and add to egg-broccoli mixture.

2 teaspoons lemon juice
1 teaspoon Worcestershire sauce
1/4 teaspoon Tabasco

4. Stir lemon juice, Worcestershire sauce and Tabasco into mixture. Pour into oiled 1½-quart ring mold and refrigerate at least 3 hours. Unmold on lettuce or other salad greens. This is good with ham or turkey buffet.

CAULIFLOWER WITH GUACAMOLE
coliflor con guacamole

Cooking Time: 6 minutes
Utensils: Paper plate
            Deep serving bowl
Servings: 6

1 (1½-lb.) whole cauliflower

1. Rinse whole cauliflower and place on a small paper plate. Cover completely with plastic wrap. Microwave on **HIGH (100%) 3 MINUTES**. Turn cauliflower package over and cook on **HIGH (100%) 3 MINUTES**. Cauliflower should be tender. Sprinkle very lightly with salt.

GUACAMOLE SAUCE:

3 ripe avocados
1 large ripe tomato, chopped
1½ Tablespoons lime or
    lemon juice
2 Tablespoons onion,
    chopped
2 teaspoons green chilies,
    seeded and chopped
2 teaspoons salt
1/2 teaspoon red pepper
1/4 teaspoon Tabasco

2. Peel avocados, (keep seed), and mash until smooth. Add tomato, lemon juice, onion, chilies, salt, pepper and Tabasco. Place half of guacamole in a deep bowl and put cooled cauliflower head down into the guacamole. Cover and chill 4 hours. Reserve remaining guacamole in small container and place seed in sauce to retard darkening of avocado. Cover and chill.

To serve, cut off stem and set cauliflower right side up on a platter of lettuce leaves. Spoon all remaining Guacamole Sauce on cauliflower. Serve lettuce, cauliflower and guacamole on individual salad or dinner plate.

Optional: Top with 1/2 cup toasted chopped walnuts.

EARLY SALAD

salade de bonne heure

Cooking Time: 11 minutes
Utensils: Microsafe plate
1 or 2-quart mixing bowl
Bacon rack
Salad bowl
Servings: 8

**1 (10-oz.) package frozen
green peas**

1. Remove outer waxed wrapper and place carton of peas on a plate. Microwave on **HIGH (100%) 4 MINUTES** (peas should be crunchy). Drain and cool.

**1/2 cup celery, thinly sliced
1/2 cup green onion tops,
thinly sliced
1/4 cup green bell pepper,
chopped
1¼ teaspoon salt
1 teaspoon sugar
1/4 teaspoon pepper (white,
red or black)
1¼ cups mayonnaise**

2. In a 1 or 2-quart bowl mix together celery, onion tops, bell pepper, salt, sugar, pepper and mayonnaise. Cover and chill.

**8 slices bacon
1 head of lettuce, well
drained and broken into
small pieces or
shredded coarsely
1 cup cherry tomatoes,
halved**

3. Place bacon on a rack and cover with wax paper. Microwave on **HIGH (100%) 7 MINUTES** until crisp. Crumble and set aside. Line bottom and sides of salad bowl with lettuce. Spoon in chilled vegetable-mayonnaise mixture. Place bacon and tomatoes on top, reserving some of each for garnish. Toss just before serving and garnish.

PEACH RICE SALAD

ensalada de arroz y melecotón

Cooking Time: 20 minutes
Utensils: 3-quart ceramic casserole
         2 or 3-quart salad bowl
Servings: 4–6

2 cups water
1 cup raw rice
1/2 teaspoon salt

1. Bring water to boil in a 3-quart casserole on **HIGH (100%) 5–6 MINUTES**. Stir in rice and salt, cover with wax paper and microwave on **HIGH (100%) 10 MINUTES**. Stir. Microwave on **HIGH (100%) 4–5 MINUTES**, until rice is light and fluffy. Chill in refrigerator or freezer.

2 cups fresh peaches, peeled
**   and sliced**
1 teaspoon ascorbic acid
**   (Fruit Fresh)**
1½ Tablespoons water

2. To help retain the natural color of the peaches, dissolve ascorbic acid in water. Add to peaches and toss to coat. Let stand 10 minutes.

1 cup celery, finely chopped
1 Tablespoon onion, minced

3. Combine 2 cups chilled rice, celery and onion in a 2 or 3-quart salad bowl.

1/4 cup vegetable oil
2 Tablespoons red wine
**   vinegar**
2 Tablespoons soy sauce
1½ teaspoons seasoned salt

4. Mix oil, vinegar, soy sauce and seasoned salt in a small bowl. Whisk until thoroughly blended. Pour over rice mixture. Mix well. Add drained peaches and toss to mix. Cover and refrigerate 1½ hours to allow flavors to blend. Serve on Romaine or crisp lettuce.

GERMAN POTATO SALAD

salade aux pommed de terre allemande

Cooking Time: 25 minutes
Utensils: 2-quart glass or plastic casserole
4-cup glass measuring cup
Servings: 6

**5 medium potatoes, peeled
and cut in half
1/4 cup water
1/4 teaspoon salt**

1. Place potatoes and salted water in a 2-quart casserole. Cover with plastic wrap and microwave on **HIGH (100%) 12 MINUTES**, rearranging potatoes after 6 minutes. Let stand covered. When cool, slice into same dish.

**5 slices bacon, diced
1/2 cup onion, chopped**

2. Fry bacon covered in a 4-cup measure on **HIGH (100%) 5 MINUTES**. Remove bacon and set aside for topping. Add onion to bacon fat. Cover. Microwave on **HIGH (100%) 3 MINUTES**.

**2 Tablespoons sugar
1 Tablespoon flour
1½ teaspoons salt
1/4 teaspoon red pepper
1/2 cup water
1/4 cup tarragon or red wine
vinegar
1 (4-oz.) jar pimiento, drained
and chopped**

3. Stir in sugar, flour, salt, red pepper, water and vinegar to cooked onions. Microwave on **HIGH (100%) 3 MINUTES**, stirring once. Pour sauce over sliced potatoes. Add pimiento and toss lightly. Cover and microwave on **HIGH (100%) 2 MINUTES**. Serve hot, topped with bacon.

SPINACH SALAD LOUISE

insalata di spinace, moda luisa

The secret of this salad is in the delicious dressing which should be prepared and refrigerated for 24 hours.

DRESSING:
Yields 1 quart

1½ Tablespoon minced onion
3 Tablespoons dry yellow
mustard
1⅓ Tablespoons salt
2/3 cup red wine vinegar
2/3 cup warm water

1. Mix onion, mustard, salt, vinegar and water in blender or food processor for 15 seconds.

1 teaspoon Worcestershire
sauce
4 dashes Tabasco
2⅓ cups vegetable oil

2. Add Worcestershire, Tabasco and with machine running, gradually add oil. Place in 1-quart container to store in refrigerator. Use 3/4 cup of dressing per pound of fresh spinach.

SALAD FOR 6:

Cooking Time: 6–7 minutes
Utensils: Bacon rack
Salad bowl

1 pound fresh spinach

1. Wash and spin dry spinach, remove stems and tear into extra large bite-size pieces.

1/2 pound bacon

2. Microwave bacon covered on a rack on **HIGH (100%) 6 to 7 MINUTES** or until crisp. Crumble.

1/2 pound fresh mushrooms,
sliced thin
1 cup toasted croutons, plain
or garlic

3. In a large salad bowl toss spinach, bacon, mushrooms and croutons. Pour 3/4 cup dressing over salad.

Desserts

Desserts:

postres Spanish
dolci Italian
dessert French

The microwave brings back old favorites, bundt cakes, flaky pie crusts, old-fashioned candies and flambé fruits to crown, with glory, any meal.

AMARETTO BUNDT CAKE

torta all'amaretto

Cooking Time: 14 minutes
Utensils: Large mixing bowl
        Large glass or ceramic bundt dish
        4-cup glass measuring cup
Servings: 12

1/2 cup ground pecans

1. Lightly grease a bundt dish and sprinkle ground pecans evenly over the bottom.

1 (18½-oz.) box Duncan Hines Deluxe II yellow cake mix
1 (3¾-oz.) box dry instant vanilla pudding
2 (7-oz.) packages almond paste, crumbled
4 eggs
1/2 cup vegetable oil
1/2 cup Amaretto liqueur
1/2 cup water

2. Blend cake mix, instant pudding and crumbled almond paste in food processor with steel blade. Transfer to large mixing bowl. Add eggs, oil, Amaretto and water. Beat with an electric beater for 4 minutes until mixture is well blended. Pour batter into prepared bundt dish. Microwave on **HIGH (100%) 11 MINUTES**, rotating dish 1/4 turn at 2 minute intervals. Cool 10 minutes while preparing glaze.

GLAZE:

1/2 cup margarine
1/2 cup sugar
1/4 cup Amaretto liqueur
1/4 cup water

3. In a 4-cup measure, melt margarine on **HIGH (100%) 1 MINUTE**. Add sugar, Amaretto and water. Bring to boil on **HIGH (100%) 2 MINUTES**. Stir once. Before removing from bundt dish make slits in cake. Pour glaze over cake in dish and let stand several hours. Turn out onto a serving plate.

BANANA RUM CAKE

torta de plátanos y ron

Cooking Time: Cake—15 minutes
Glaze—3 minutes 30 seconds
Utensils: Large ceramic bundt dish
4-cup glass measuring cup
Servings: 10–12

1 Tablespoon sugar
1 teaspoon cinnamon

1. Lightly grease a large bundt dish with margarine. Mix together sugar and cinnamon and sprinkle in bundt dish.

1 (18½-oz.) Duncan Hines Butter Recipe Golden Cake Mix
1 (3⅛-oz.) package vanilla pudding and pie filling mix (not instant)
4 eggs
1/2 cup vegetable oil
1/2 cup buttermilk
1½ teaspoon vanilla
1 cup mashed bananas
1 cup chopped pecans

2. In a large mixing bowl and using an electric beater, combine cake mix, pudding mix, eggs, vegetable oil, buttermilk and vanilla until thoroughly blended. Add mashed bananas and pecans. Pour into prepared bundt dish. Microwave on **MEDIUM (50%) 10 MINUTES** and then on **HIGH (100%) 5 MINUTES**. Rotate dish 4 times. Let cool slightly.

3. While cake is still warm and in the dish, spoon Rum Glaze over it. Let sit in pan for 30 minutes before turning out on a large serving dish.

RUM GLAZE:

1/2 cup margarine
1 cup sugar
1/4 cup rum, light or dark

4. Melt margarine in a 4-cup measure on **HIGH (100%) 1 MINUTE**. Stir in sugar and rum. Mix well. Microwave on **HIGH (100%) 2 MINUTES 30 SECONDS**.

BIRD OF PARADISE CAKE

torta del ave de paraíso

Cooking Time: 10 minutes per layer
Utensils: 2 (9-inch) round glass cake dishes
Servings: 12

2 cups sugar
3 cups all-purpose flour
1 teaspoon soda
1 teaspoon ground cinnamon
1 teaspoon salt
3 eggs, beaten
1½ cups vegetable oil
1½ teaspoons vanilla extract
1 (8-oz.) can crushed
    pineapple, drained
2 cups chopped pecans, or
    walnuts, divided
2 cups bananas, mashed

1. Mix sugar, flour, soda, cinnamon and salt in a large mixing bowl. Add eggs and oil, stirring until dry ingredients are moistened. Do not beat. Stir in vanilla, drained pineapple, 1 cup chopped nuts and bananas. Spoon batter into 2 (9-inch) cake dishes lined on bottom with wax paper. Microwave **each** layer on **MEDIUM (50%) 7 MINUTES**. Then microwave on **HIGH (100%) 3 MINUTES**, rotating dish 2 or 3 times. Remove from dishes after 10 minutes standing time and cool completely before frosting.

FROSTING:

1 (8-oz.) package cream
    cheese, softened
1/2 cup margarine, softened
1 (16-oz.) package
    confectioners powdered
    sugar
1 teaspoon vanilla extract

2. Combine cream cheese and margarine, cream until smooth. Add sugar, beating until light and fluffy. Stir in vanilla. Spread frosting between layers and on top and sides of cake. Sprinkle top with remaining 1 cup nuts. Refrigerate cake.

CARROT CAKE LORRAINE

torta di carote, moda lorraine

Cooking Time: 15 minutes
Utensils: 12-cup ceramic Bundt dish
2-cup glass measuring cup
Servings: 12–16

**1 Tablespoon granulated
sugar**
1 teaspoon cinnamon

1. Lightly grease a 12-cup bundt dish with margarine. Mix together sugar and cinnamon and sprinkle in bundt dish.

**1 (18½-oz.) package Pillsbury
Plus Yellow Cake Mix**
3 eggs
1/3 cup vegetable oil
1/2 cup water
2 teaspoons cinnamon
**1/3 cup firmly packed brown
sugar**

2. In a large mixing bowl combine cake mix, eggs, oil, water, cinnamon and brown sugar. Blend with a wire whisk or electric hand mixer.

2 cups shredded carrots
1/2 cup raisins
1/2 cup pecans, chopped

GLAZE:

**1 cup powdered
confectioners sugar**
**1½ ounces cream cheese,
softened**
2 Tablespoons milk
1 teaspoon vanilla

3. Fold in carrots, raisins and nuts. Pour batter into prepared bundt dish. Microwave on **MEDIUM (50%) 10 MINUTES**, rotating dish at 5 minute intervals. Then microwave on **HIGH (100%) 5 MINUTES**. Test with wooden pick. An additional minute on High may be needed. Place on a wooden board to cool 10 minutes. Prepare glaze while cake cools. Mix cream cheese, milk, vanilla and powdered sugar together in a 2-cup measure. Invert cake onto plate and frost with glaze.

189

CHERRY CRUMBLE

Cooking Time: 14 to 15 minutes
Utensil: 7 x 11-inch glass baking dish
Servings: 12

1 (18½-oz.) box yellow cake mix
1 (21-oz.) can cherry pie filling

1. Remove 1 cup of cake mix from box and reserve for topping. Sprinkle remaining dry cake mix (3 cups) in a greased 7 x 11-inch glass baking dish. Spread cherry pie filling over cake mix. Sprinkle reserved cake mix over pie filling.

1/2 cup water
1 teaspoon lemon juice
1/2 teaspoon cinnamon

2. Combine water and lemon juice. Pour evenly over mix. Sprinkle with cinnamon. Microwave on **HIGH (100%) 14–15 MINUTES**. Rotate dish 2 times.
   Serve warm or cold. Nice with ice cream.

MICRO MEMO:

If one area of the cake has not cooked as quickly as the rest, place a sheet of foil under the dish in this area while it stands on the counter top.

CHOCOLATE CAKE

gâteau de chocolat quimper

Cooking Time: 10 minutes per layer
Utensils: 2 (9-inch) glass or plastic cake dishes
        1-cup measuring cup
        Large mixing bowl
Servings: 24

3 (1-oz.) semi-sweet
    chocolate squares,
    melted
1⅔ cup crème fraîche
3 eggs, beaten
1 teaspoon almond extract or
    Amaretto
2¼ cups sifted all-purpose
    flour
1/8 teaspoon salt
2¼ teaspoons baking powder
1½ cups sugar

1. Melt chocolate squares in a 1-cup measure on **HIGH (100%) 2 MIN-UTES**. In a large bowl mix together crème fraîche (see page 43), chocolate, eggs and Amaretto. Add sifted flour, salt, baking powder and sugar. Beat together well. Pour into 2 (9-inch) cake dishes lined with wax paper on the bottom; do not grease sides. Cook **each** layer on **MEDIUM (50%) 7 MINUTES**, turning at 2-minute intervals. Continue to cook on **HIGH (100%) 3 MIN-UTES**. Cool 10 minutes, turn out on a plate. Split each layer in half with a taut string or slice with a knife. Cool then frost.

FROSTING:

2 cups crème fraîche
1/2 cup confectioners
    powdered sugar
1½ teaspoon almond extract
    or Amaretto

2. Mix crème fraîche, powdered sugar and almond extract together. Spread frosting on each layer (not sides). Stack the layers. Top with frosting.

CHOCOLATE PECAN BUNDT CAKE
torta de chocolate y pacanas

Cooking Time: 16 minutes
Utensils: Large ceramic bundt dish
2-cup glass measuring cup
1½-quart glass mixing bowl
Servings: 12–15

Margarine
1 Tablespoon sugar

1. Grease a large bundt dish with margarine and sprinkle with sugar to coat dish.

1/2 cup margarine
2 cups sugar
1 (6-oz.) package semi-sweet chocolate chips
2 eggs, beaten

2. Cream margarine and sugar in a large mixing bowl. In a 2-cup measure melt chocolate chips on **HIGH (100%) 1–1½ MINUTES**, stirring once. Add chocolate and eggs to creamed mixture.

2 cups all-purpose flour
1½ teaspoons baking powder
1½ cups milk
1 teaspoon vanilla
1 cup chopped pecans or walnuts

3. Sift flour and baking powder together. Add alternately with milk to chocolate mixture. Add vanilla and nuts. Mix well. Pour into prepared bundt dish and microwave on **MEDIUM (50%) 9 MINUTES** rotating dish at 5 minutes. Continue to microwave on **HIGH (100%) 4 MINUTES**. Use a cake tester or wooden pick to check for doneness. Invert on a wire rack after standing 10 minutes. Freeze or refrigerate cake 30 minutes before frosting.

FROSTING:

2 (1-oz.) squares semi-sweet chocolate
1/2 cup margarine, softened
1 egg, beaten
1 teaspoon lemon juice
1½ cups powdered confectioners sugar
1 cup finely chopped pecans or walnuts

4. Melt chocolate in a 1½-quart glass mixing bowl on **HIGH (100%) 1 MINUTE 30 SECONDS** stirring at 30 second intervals. Stir until melted. While chocolate is hot, beat in softened margarine and egg. Add lemon juice. Sift in powdered sugar. Beat until well blended. Stir in nuts. Frost cake and refrigerate.

MINT CHOCOLATE SQUARES

morceaux chocolats au menthe

Cooking Time: 10 minutes
Utensils: 2-cup glass measuring cup
         7 x 11-inch glass baking dish
         1-quart glass casserole
Servings: Makes 5 dozen or more

FIRST LAYER:

**2 (1-oz.) squares
   unsweetened chocolate
1/2 cup margarine
2 eggs
1 cup sugar
1/2 cup all-purpose flour
1 cup pecans, chopped**

SECOND LAYER:

**2 cups confectioners
   powdered sugar
3 Tablespoons margarine,
   softened
2 Tablespoons whipping
   cream
3/4 teaspoon pure mint and
   peppermint extract
4 drops green food coloring**

THIRD LAYER:

**1½ cups milk chocolate chips
3 Tablespoons vegetable
   shortening (not butter
   or margarine)**

1. Melt chocolate and margarine in a 2-cup measure on **HIGH (100%) 1 MINUTE**. Cool. Beat eggs and sugar in a small bowl until light and thick. Stir in flour, pecans and melted chocolate. Spoon mixture into a greased 7 x 11-inch baking dish. Microwave on **HIGH (100%) 5–6 MINUTES**, rotate dish 2 times. Let stand on counter to firm. Cool.

2. Using the back of a spoon combine powdered sugar, margarine, cream, mint extract, and green food coloring until smooth. Spread and pat evenly over baked layer.

3. Place chocolate and shortening in a 1-quart casserole or bowl. Cover with plastic wrap. Microwave on **MEDIUM (50%) 2½–3 MINUTES** until most of the chips are shiny and soft. Stir and spread over mint layer. Cover with plastic wrap and chill. Cut into 1/2-inch or 1-inch squares.

CICI'S CRÈME DE MENTHE CAKE

gateau crème de menthe cici

Cooking Time: 15 minutes
Utensil: Large microwave bundt dish
Servings: 12

1 (18½-oz.) package white
   cake mix, sifted
1 (3¾-oz.) package instant
   vanilla pudding and pie
   filling
4 large eggs, beaten
1/2 cup orange juice
1/2 cup vegetable oil
1/4 cup water
1/4 cup Crème de Menthe
1/4 teaspoon vanilla
2 drops green food coloring

1 (5½-oz.) can chocolate
   syrup
Chocolate sprinkles or
   miniature chocolate
   chips

1. Grease bottom of large ceramic bundt dish. Place cake mix and dry pudding mix in food processor with steel blade. Process on/off several times to mix and sift the dry ingredients. Transfer to an 8-cup measure and stir in beaten eggs, orange juice, oil, water, Crème de Menthe, vanilla and green food coloring. Mix well. Pour two-thirds of batter (2⅔ cups) in bundt dish.

2. Mix chocolate syrup into remaining batter in mixing bowl. Pour chocolate mixture over Crème de Menthe mixture in bundt dish, but do not stir into batter. Microwave on **MEDIUM (50%) 10 MINUTES**, rotating dish a 1/4 turn 3 times. Continue to microwave on **HIGH (100%) 4–5 MINUTES**, rotating dish once. Use a cake tester to test for doneness. Let stand on counter 10 minutes before inverting onto cake plate. Decorate with chocolate sprinkles.

HEAVENLY HASH CAKE

Cooking Time: 12 minutes
Utensils: 7 x 11-inch glass baking dish
　　　　　1-quart glass mixing bowl
Servings: 32 squares

1/2 cup margarine
1 cup sugar
2 eggs
2 Tablespoons cocoa
3/4 cup self-rising flour
1 cup pecans, chopped
1 teaspoon vanilla

1. Cream margarine in a mixing bowl. Beat in sugar, eggs, cocoa, flour, pecans and vanilla. Pour into a greased 7 x 11-inch glass baking dish. Microwave on **MEDIUM (50%) 7 MINUTES**, rotating dish every 2 minutes. Then microwave on **HIGH (100%) 3 MINUTES**, rotating dish once.

1 (10½-oz.) bag of miniature
**　marshmallows, enough**
**　to cover cake**

2. While hot, cover cake with marshmallows. Let cake stand 5 minutes while preparing icing.

ICING:

1 pound box confectioners
**　powdered sugar**
1/2 cup cocoa
1/3 cup milk
1 Tablespoon vanilla

3. Mix powdered sugar and cocoa in a 1-quart mixing bowl. Add milk. Microwave on **HIGH (100%) 2 MINUTES**. Stir in vanilla and pour icing over cake.

OATMEAL CAKE

gateau au farine d'avoine

Stays moist for days

Cooking Time: 19 minutes
Utensils: Large ceramic bundt dish
        8-cup glass measuring cup
        1-quart glass bowl
Servings: 12

1 Tablespoon sugar
1 teaspoon cinnamon

1. Butter the bundt dish and sprinkle with mixture of cinnamon and sugar.

1¼ cup boiling water
1 cup regular oatmeal

2. In an 8-cup measure bring water to boil on **HIGH (100%) 3 MINUTES**. Stir in oats and let stand 20 minutes.

1 cup brown sugar
1 cup margarine
2 eggs, slightly beaten
1⅓ cups all-purpose flour
1 teaspoon soda
1/2 teaspoon salt
2 teaspoons cinnamon
1 teaspoon vanilla

3. Add brown sugar, margarine, eggs, flour, soda, salt, cinnamon and vanilla. Beat well and pour into the prepared bundt dish. Microwave on **MEDIUM (50%) for 10 MINUTES.** Turn at 5-minute intervals. Microwave on **HIGH (100%) 4 MINUTES.** Invert cake onto plate and let stand 10 minutes before removing cake dish. Frost while warm.

FROSTING:

1/2 cup pecans, chopped
1/2 cup coconut, grated
1 cup brown sugar
1/2 cup evaporated milk
1 teaspoon vanilla

4. Mix pecans and coconut in a 1-quart bowl. Microwave on **HIGH (100%) 2 MINUTES**, stirring at 1 minute. Add brown sugar, milk and vanilla. Mix well and spread on cake.

PINEAPPLE UPSIDE DOWN CAKE

torta de piña al revés

Cooking Time: 14 minutes
Utensils: 10-inch micro plastic or glass cake dish
with 2-inch sides
2 mixing bowls
Servings: 12

1/4 cup margarine
2/3 cup brown sugar, firmly packed
1 (14-oz.) can sliced pineapple, well drained, reserve liquid
6 maraschino cherries, well drained
Pecan halves

1. Cut a circle of wax paper to fit bottom of a 10-inch cake dish. Melt margarine in the lined dish on **HIGH (100%) 1 MINUTE**. Sprinkle in brown sugar. Next arrange pineapple slices, cherries and pecans on top of brown sugar.

2 cups all-purpose flour
2 teaspoons baking powder
1/8 teaspoon salt
1/2 cup margarine
1½ cups sugar
3/4 cup pineapple juice

2. Sift flour, baking powder and salt. In the food processor or with a hand mixer cream margarine. Add sugar through the feeder tube and process until light and fluffy. Add 4 tablespoons flour at a time and alternate with pineapple juice until mixed. Do not over mix (use short on/off pulses).

4 egg whites
1/4 teaspoon cream of tartar
1 teaspoon vanilla

3. In another mixing bowl beat egg whites, cream of tartar and vanilla until stiff. Fold into cake batter and pour batter into prepared dish. Microwave on **MEDIUM (50%) 7 MINUTES**. Turn dish and microwave on **HIGH (100%) 6 MINUTES**, turning dish at three minutes. Test cake with wooden pick. An additional minute on High may be needed to firm the center. Invert the dish onto a serving plate after 10 minutes.

CLOUD "9" PIE FILLING

relleno de "nube 9"

A light lemony dessert

Cooking Time: 4 minutes 30 seconds
Utensils: 9-inch glass pie plate
           4-cup glass measuring cup
Servings: 12

1 (9-inch) pastry shell, baked

1. Prepare your favorite pastry, 9-inch shell or 12 individual tart shells.

3 Tablespoons cornstarch
3/4 cup sugar
1 cup water
1 teaspoon lemon zest
    (grated rind)
1/3 cup lemon juice
2 egg yolks, slightly beaten
1 (3-oz.) package cream
    cheese, softened

2. Mix cornstarch and sugar in a 4-cup measure. Stir in water, lemon zest, lemon juice and egg yolks. Beat until well blended. Microwave on **HIGH (100%) 4 MINUTES 30 SECONDS** until thickened. Stir in softened cream cheese until well blended. Cool mixture to room temperature before beating egg whites in the next step.

2 egg whites
1/4 cup sugar

3. Beat egg whites in a small cool mixing bowl until foamy. Add 1/4 cup sugar, gradually, beating until meringue stands in stiff glossy peaks. Fold cooled lemon mixture into meringue. Spoon lemon mixture into 12 pastry tart shells or 1 large pastry shell. Chill 2 hours before serving. May also be served in sherbet dishes.

IMPOSSIBLE PIE
torta impossible

Cooking Time: 7 minutes
Utensils: 9-inch glass or ceramic pie plate
Servings: 6 to 8

1/2 cup Bisquick
1/2 cup sugar
4 eggs
1 cup coconut
5 Tablespoons margarine
1 teaspoon vanilla
1½ cups milk

1. Quickly blend Bisquick, sugar, eggs, coconut and margarine in food processor or blender. Add vanilla and milk. Process a few seconds until mixed well.

2. Pour into a greased 9-inch pie plate. Microwave on **HIGH (100%) 7 MINUTES**. Rotate dish several times for more even cooking. Let stand 10 minutes on counter top before chilling in refrigerator.

CHERRY CHEESECAKE CUPS

Cooking Time: 3 minutes
Utensils: 1-quart glass mixing bowl
         Micro-muffin pan
         6 paper cupcake liners
Servings: 6

**1 (8-oz.) package cream
   cheese**

1. Soften cream cheese in a 1-quart mixing bowl on **MEDIUM (50%) 1 MINUTE**.

**1/3 cup sugar
1 egg
1 Tablespoon lemon juice
1 teaspoon vanilla**

2. Beat in sugar, egg, lemon juice and vanilla until light and fluffy.

6 vanilla wafers

3. Line a micro-muffin pan (or 6 custard cups) with paper liners. Place a vanilla wafer in bottom of each liner and fill 3/4 full with the cream cheese mixture. Cook 6 cheesecake cups on **MEDIUM (50%) 2 MINUTES**, or until nearly set, rotating dish once.

Canned cherry pie filling

4. Top each with 2 tablespoons of pie filling. Chill.

Cherry Cheesecake Cups may be frozen separately and then stored in a plastic bag for a quick dessert. Pineapple, blueberry or strawberry pie filling may be substituted. Also try a chocolate cookie in place of the vanilla wafer sometime!

PUMPKIN CHEESECAKE
tarte au fromage blanc parfumée au citrouille

Cooking Time: 12 minutes
Utensils: 9-inch round cake or pie dish
2-cup glass measuring cup
1-quart glass measure or dish
Servings: 10–12

CRUST:

1/4 cup melted butter or margarine
1 cup graham cracker crumbs
1/2 teaspoon cinnamon

1. Spray bottom of cake or pie dish with a non-stick spray (Pam). In a 2-cup glass measure melt butter. Add graham crackers and cinnamon. Stir until mixed. Press to bottom of cake dish. Cook on **HIGH (100%) 2 MINUTES**. Turn at 1 minute. Cool.

FILLING:

3 eggs
12 ounces cream cheese
3/4 cup sugar
1½ Tablespoons all-purpose flour
3/4 teaspoon grated orange rind
3/4 teaspoon grated lemon rind
1 cup canned pumpkin
1/2 teaspoon vanilla

2. Place eggs in food processor (steel blade). Process with 2 or 3 quick on/offs. Add all the cream cheese (cut in chunks), sugar, flour and fruit rinds. Process with several quick on/offs then blend until smooth. Add pumpkin and vanilla. Process quickly to mix. Pour into a 1-quart dish. Cook on **HIGH (100%) 4 MINUTES** stirring every minute. Pour into crust. Cook on **HIGH (100%) 4 MINUTES** or until filling is puffed around edges. Cool 5 minutes.

TOPPING:

1½ cups sour cream
2 Tablespoons sugar
1/2 teaspoon vanilla

3. Combine sour cream, sugar and vanilla. Spread over top. Cook on **HIGH (100%) 2 MINUTES**. Chill 5 hours before serving.

OLD-FASHIONED VINEGAR PIE

tarte de vinaigre d'autre-fois

Cooking Time: 6 minutes
Utensils: 9-inch glass pie plate
8-cup glass measuring cup
Servings: 12

1 (9-inch) pie shell, baked

1. Follow directions on page 203 for Pie Crust II.

1/2 cup margarine, melted and cooled
1½ cups sugar
2 Tablespoons flour
1 Tablespoon vanilla extract
2 Tablespoons vinegar
3 eggs

2. In an 8-cup measure beat margarine and sugar until fluffy. Add flour, vanilla, vinegar and eggs, one at a time. If mixture separates while beating, it will become smooth while microwaving.

3. Microwave mixture on **HIGH (100%) 4 MINUTES**, stirring at 1-minute intervals until thickened. Pour into baked pie shell and microwave on **HIGH (100%) 2 MINUTES** until set. Serve at room temperature or chilled.

QUICHE PASTRY

With food processor

Cooking Time: 5–6 minutes
Utensils: 10-inch ceramic quiche dish
Servings: 1 (9 or 10-inch) crust

1 cup all-purpose flour, unsifted
1/2 teaspoon salt
3 Tablespoons shortening
3 Tablespoons cold margarine

1. Using the steel blade, place flour, salt, shortening and margarine in bowl. Process on/off until coarse.

2½ Tablespoons ice water
3 drops yellow food coloring

(As an alternative to food coloring, try brushing a mixture of 1 egg yolk and 1 teaspoon of Worcestershire sauce over all the crust before baking!)

2. Blend water and food coloring. Pour into feeder tube with machine running. Stop machine when dough forms a ball on top of blade. Do **not** overprocess. Remove from bowl. Knead 3 times. Roll into ball. Roll out between 2 sheets of wax paper to fit a 9 or 10-inch quiche dish. Prick shell with fork. Microwave on **HIGH (100%) 5–6 MINUTES**. Rotate dish two times.

BUTTERMILK CHESS PIE

tarte de babeurre

Cooking Time: 8 minutes
Utensils: 9-inch glass pie plate
8-cup glass measuring cup
Servings: 12

1 (9-inch) pie shell, baked

1. Prepare your favorite pastry or follow directions below for Pie Crust II.

3 eggs
1½ cups sugar
2 Tablespoons all-purpose flour
Pinch of salt
1/2 cup margarine, melted
1/2 cup buttermilk
2 Tablespoons lemon juice
1 teaspoon grated lemon rind
1/2 teaspoon vanilla

2. In an 8-cup measure beat eggs. Add sugar, flour and salt. Mix well. Beat in melted margarine and add buttermilk. Gradually add lemon juice, rind and vanilla. If mixture separates while beating, it will become smooth while microwaving. Microwave on **HIGH (100%) 6 MINUTES**, stirring at 2-minute intervals. Pour mixture into baked pie shell. Microwave on **HIGH (100%) 1 to 2 MINUTES** until set. Rotate dish once.

PIE CRUST II

For food processor or by hand

Cooking Time: 5–6 minutes
Utensils: 9 or 10-inch glass pie plate
Servings: 1 (9 or 10-inch) pie crust

2 cups all-purpose flour
1½ teaspoon salt
1/2 cup vegetable oil
1/4 cup cold whole milk plus 3
**   drops yellow food coloring**

Using the steel blade, sift flour and salt in food processor with 2 quick on/offs. Pour in oil, milk and food coloring. Process until dough forms a ball on top of blade. Roll out dough between two sheets of wax paper to fit a 9 or 10-inch glass pie plate. Prick shell with fork. Microwave on **HIGH (100%) 5 to 6 MINUTES**. Rotate dish two times.

MICRO MEMO:

After pricking bottom and sides of pie shell, rub a mixture of 1½ teaspoons flour and 1½ teaspoons sugar into holes. This keeps crust from becoming soggy.

KING KAMEHAMEHA PIE

Pronounced kah-may-ah-may-ah

Cooking time: 13 minutes
Utensils: Glass pie plate
         Plastic or glass cake dish
         2-cup glass measuring cup
Servings: 10–12

1 (9-inch) pie shell

1. Bake pie shell according to directions on page 203.

6 medium golden apples, peeled, cored and cut into wedges
1/2 cup pineapple juice

2. Cut apples into approximately 36 wedges. Place in a cake dish with 1/2 cup pineapple juice. Cover and microwave on **HIGH (100%) 7–8 MINUTES** until apples are tender. Drain and reserve 1/2 cup liquid. Keep covered.

1 cup pineapple juice
3/4 cup sugar

3. In a 2-cup measure mix pineapple juice and sugar together. Microwave on **HIGH (100%) 3 MINUTES 30 SECONDS** until mixture comes to a boil.

3 Tablespoons cornstarch
1 Tablespoon butter
1/2 teaspoon vanilla
1/2 teaspoon salt
1 cup whipped cream
1/2 cup chopped macadamia nuts

4. Add cornstarch to reserved 1/2 cup pineapple juice to make a paste. Stir into the boiling juice. Cook on **HIGH (100%) 1 MINUTE 30 SECONDS**, stirring every 30 seconds until thick. Add butter, vanilla and salt. Cool 10 minutes. Pour half of the syrup into pie shell. Arrange two layers of apples in a wheel design. Spoon remaining syrup over apples. Chill. Garnish center of pie with whipped cream and chopped macadamia nuts.

PEACH OF A PIE

pastel melocotón de lujo

Cooking Time: 4 minutes 30 seconds
Utensils: 9-inch glass pie plate
          Small mixing bowl
          2-cup glass measuring cup
Servings: 6–8

1 (9-inch) pie shell, baked

1. Prepare your favorite pastry or follow directions on page 203.

1/4 cup sugar
2 Tablespoons cornstarch
1 Tablespoon lemon juice
1 (10-oz.) package frozen strawberries, thawed with liquid (do not drain)

2. Mix sugar and cornstarch together in a 2-cup measure. Stir in lemon juice and thawed strawberries. Microwave on **HIGH (100%) 4 MINUTES 30 SECONDS**. Stir at 2 minutes, then every minute until thickened. Cool. For quick cooling pour mixture into another dish and place in the freezer for a few minutes.

1 (8-oz.) package cream cheese
1/4 cup sugar
1/4 teaspoon salt
1 Tablespoon milk
1/2 teaspoon vanilla extract

3. In a small bowl mix cream cheese until soft and creamy. Add sugar, salt, milk and vanilla; blend thoroughly. Spread the cheese mixture on bottom and sides of cool pie shell.

1 (1-lb. 13-oz.) can cling peach slices, drained
Whipped cream

4. Spoon 1/3 of the cooled strawberry mixture over cream cheese. Arrange well-drained peach slices over pie and top with remaining strawberry mixture. Refrigerate until firm. Garnish with whipped cream.

DORA'S CHOCOLATE PECAN PIE

pastel de chocolate y pecanas a la dora

Cooking Time: 10 minutes 30 seconds
Utensils: 9-inch glass pie plate
4-cup glass measuring cup
Mixing bowl
Servings: 10–12

1 (9-inch) pie shell, baked

1. Prepare your favorite pastry or follow directions on page 203.

**2 (1-oz.) squares
unsweetened chocolate
3 Tablespoons margarine
1 cup light corn syrup
3/4 cup sugar**

2. In a 4-cup measure melt chocolate and margarine on **HIGH (100%) 1 MINUTE 30 SECONDS**. Stir after one minute. Add syrup and sugar, mix well. Microwave on **HIGH (100%) 2 MINUTES**. Cool.

**3 eggs
1 teaspoon vanilla
1 cup pecans, chopped
1/2 cup whipping cream**

3. Beat eggs slightly in a mixing bowl. Slowly pour chocolate over eggs, stirring constantly. Add vanilla and nuts and pour into baked pie shell. Microwave on **HIGH (100%) 7 MINUTES**, turning every 2 minutes. Cool. Top with whipped cream before serving.

PETITE CRANBERRY TASSIES

A Christmas treat cooked in paper egg cartons

Cooking Time: 8 minutes, 20 seconds
Utensils: 1-quart glass bowl
          1 paper egg carton
          24 miniature paper liners
Servings: 2 dozen tassies

**1 (3-oz.) package cream
    cheese
1/2 cup margarine
1 cup sifted all-purpose flour**

1. Soften cream cheese and margarine in a 1-quart bowl on **HIGH (100%) 10–20 SECONDS**. Blend, then add flour. Chill pastry then roll into 2 dozen 1-inch balls. Press dough on bottom then up sides of 24 tiny muffin paper liners. Place 12 in a paper egg carton (plastic carton may be used as a second choice). Microwave on **HIGH (100%) 2 MINUTES**, rotating egg carton at 1 minute.

FILLING:

**1 egg
1 Tablespoon soft margarine
3/4 cup brown sugar
1 teaspoon vanilla extract
Dash of salt
1/3 cup cranberries, fresh or
    frozen, finely chopped
3 Tablespoons pecans,
    coarsely broken**

2. Beat together egg, margarine, brown sugar, vanilla and salt. Stir in cranberries and nuts. Place 1 heaping teaspoon in baked shells. Microwave 12 in one carton on **HIGH (100%) 2 MINUTES**, rotating carton once. Remove from carton and repeat cooking procedure with remaining tassies. When cool, remove from paper liners.

207

PECAN PIE

tarte de pacanes

Cooking Time: 16 minutes
Utensils: 9-inch glass pie plate
           3-quart glass bowl
           1-quart mixing bowl
Servings: 8–10

1 (9-inch) pie shell, baked

1. Bake your favorite pastry or follow directions on page 203.

1 cup dark brown sugar, packed
1 cup light corn syrup

2. In a 3-quart bowl mix brown sugar and syrup. Microwave on **HIGH (100%) 3 MINUTES** until boiling. Stir. Continue to boil on **HIGH (100%) 2 MINUTES**.

3 eggs
1/3 cup margarine
1 Tablespoon arrowroot
Pinch of salt
1 Tablespoon vanilla
1½ cups pecan halves

3. In a 1-quart bowl whisk eggs well and gradually pour hot syrup mixture into eggs, whisking constantly. Add margarine, arrowroot, salt, vanilla and pecans. Mix and pour into baked pie shell. Microwave on **MEDIUM-HIGH (70%) 10–11 MINUTES** until set. Cool before slicing.

MICRO MEMO:

Arrowroot, which resembles cornstarch, is a fine white powder which comes from the root of a tropical plant. It is more easily digested than any other starch and has a lighter and more interesting taste.

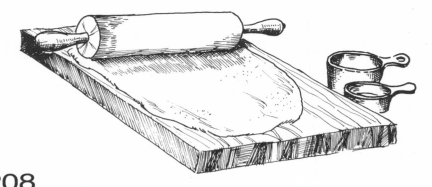

BANANAS CALYPSO

With rum sauce

Cooking Time: Rum Sauce 1¾ minutes
Bananas 7 minutes
Utensils: 3-quart glass casserole
2-cup glass measuring cup
Servings: 8

RUM SAUCE: (To be prepared and chilled first)

2 large eggs, separated
1/2 cup powdered
  confectioners sugar,
  sifted
1/4 cup light cream (half and
  half)
1/4 teaspoon salt
1 ounce Jamaican rum

1. Separate eggs and reserve whites. In a 2-cup measure beat yolks until thick. Add sugar, cream and salt. Mix well and microwave on **HIGH (100%) 1 MINUTE 45 SECONDS** or until thick, stirring every 30 seconds. Stir in rum gradually and continue beating until smooth. Chill.

2. Just before serving beat egg whites until stiff and fold into chilled sauce.

BANANAS:

1 Tablespoon butter
1/2 cup brown sugar, packed
1/4 teaspoon ground cloves
2 Tablespoons orange zest
  (grated rind)
3/4 cup orange juice

8 bananas, peeled, cut in half
  and each half split into 3
  sections. After cutting
  the bananas in half,
  gently squeeze the cut
  end and the banana will
  open into three natural
  sections.

1. Melt butter in a 3-quart casserole on **HIGH (100%) 40–60 SECONDS**. Stir in brown sugar, cloves, orange zest and juice. Microwave on **HIGH (100%) 3 MINUTES**.

2. Prepare bananas while orange mixture is cooking. Add bananas and continue cooking on **HIGH (100%) 3 MINUTES**. Stir and rearrange bananas one time. Serve warm with chilled rum sauce.

A delightfully light dessert to be served in stemmed sherbets or informally in ramekins and topped with a dollop of rum sauce.

TRUE BLUEBERRY DELIGHT

Cooking Time: 6 minutes
Utensils: 7 x 11-inch glass baking dish
          4-cup glass measuring cup
Servings: 10

PECAN CRUST:

1 cup flour
1/2 cup brown sugar
1 cup margarine
1/2 cup chopped pecans

FILLING:

1 (15-oz.) can blueberries, in
**   light syrup, drained**
2/3 cup sugar
3 Tablespoons cornstarch

2 (1½-oz.) packages Dream
**   Whip or dry dessert**
**   topping**
1 cup milk or water
1 teaspoon almond extract
1 cup powdered
**   confectioners sugar**
1 (8-oz.) package cream
**   cheese, softened**

1. Combine flour, brown sugar, and margarine. Mix together until blended. Stir in pecans. Spread on the bottom of a 7 x 11-inch greased baking dish. Microwave on **HIGH (100%) 3 MINUTES 30 SECONDS**. Rotate dish 1/2 turn after half the cooking time. Cool.

2. Drain blueberries well and reserve juice. In a 4-cup measure mix sugar and cornstarch. Slowly add blueberry juice and stir well so mixture will not lump. Microwave on **HIGH (100%) 2 MINUTES 30 SECONDS**. Stir twice during cooking time. Gently stir in blueberries and set aside to cool in the refrigerator.

3. Whip dessert topping and milk or water as directed on package. Mix in almond extract, powdered sugar and softened cream cheese. Blend until smooth and pour over cooled crust. Top with cooled blueberry mixture and chill 3 to 4 hours before serving.

FIG JAM

Cooking Time: 13 minutes
Utensils: 4-quart ceramic casserole
5 sterilized 8-ounce jars
Servings: Makes 5 cups

3 cups, fresh figs, puréed
1 (3-oz.) package lemon
flavored gelatin
1 (3-oz.) package apricot
flavored gelatin
2½ cups sugar

Purée figs in food processor and combine with gelatin and sugar in a 4-quart casserole. Stir well. Cover and microwave on **HIGH (100%) 10 MINUTES** until boiling, stirring at 5-minute intervals. Continue to microwave on **HIGH (100%) 3 MINUTES**. Pour into sterilized jars and seal immediately.

SPARKLING PINK CHAMPAGNE JELLY

Cooking Time: 9–10 minutes
Utensils: 3-quart glass casserole
4 (8-oz.) Kerr jars
Servings: 4

1¾ cups pink champagne
3 cups sugar

1. Stir together champagne and sugar in a 3-quart glass casserole. Cover. Microwave on **HIGH (100%) 4 MINUTES**. Stir. Continue to microwave on **HIGH (100%) 4–5 MINUTES** until mixture boils. Let mixture boil 1 minute more. Stir.

3 ounces Certo liquid fruit
pectin

2. Add liquid fruit pectin gradually to hot mixture, mixing well. If necessary remove foam with metal spoon. Pour into sterilized Kerr Old Country Kitchen 8-ounce jars. Wipe top of jar clean with paper towel. Put on scalded lids and seal. Refrigerate.

PEACHES BIGGS FLAMBÉ

pêches flambées biggs

Over ice cream

Cooking Time: 7 minutes
Utensils: 2-quart glass dish
Servings: 8

1/2 cup margarine
1/2 cup brown sugar
1/2 teaspoon ground
cinnamon

1. Melt margarine in a 2-quart dish on **HIGH (100%) 1 MINUTE**. Stir in brown sugar and cinnamon. Microwave on **HIGH (100%) 2 MINUTES**, stirring after the first minute.

4 ripe peaches, peeled, pitted
and cut in 1/4-inch slices

2. Add peaches and baste with syrup. Microwave on **HIGH (100%) 4 MINUTES**. Stir at 1-minute intervals.

1/2 cup peach brandy
1/2 cup rum, 151 proof for
flaming

3. Pour peach brandy and rum over warm peaches. Pour a small amount of rum in a large metal spoon. Ignite rum in the spoon and tip spoon into peach mixture to ignite. Have a metal lid handy in case it is too flambé. Spoon peaches and sauce over ice cream. Serve immediately.

FRESH PEACH COBBLER

With dumplings

Cooking Time: 18 minutes
Utensils: 8 or 9-inch round glass cake dish
              1-quart glass bowl
Servings: 6

1½ Tablespoons arrowroot
1/3 cup brown sugar
1/3 cup water
4 cups fresh peaches, peeled
    and sliced
1 Tablespoon margarine
1 Tablespoon lemon juice

1. Mix arrowroot and brown sugar in a round cake dish. Stir in water. Add peaches and stir gently. Microwave on **HIGH (100%) 6–8 MINUTES** until mixture boils and thickens. Stir 1 or 2 times. After mixture thickens stir in margarine and lemon juice. Prepare dumpling batter while peaches are cooking.

DUMPLING BATTER:

2 Tablespoons margarine
1 egg
1/2 cup all-purpose flour
1/2 cup sugar
1/2 teaspoon baking powder
1/4 teaspoon salt
1/2 Tablespoon sugar
1/2 Tablespoon cinnamon

2. Soften margarine in a 1-quart bowl on **HIGH (100%) 10–20 SECONDS** or over a bowl of warm water. Beat in egg. Add flour, sugar, baking powder and salt. Beat with spoon until batter is smooth. Drop batter by spoonfuls in a circle over hot peach mixture (about 6–8 drops). Sprinkle a mixture of sugar and cinnamon over batter. Microwave on **HIGH (100%) 10 MINUTES**. During the last 2 minutes of cooking, spoon hot peach syrup over dumplings. Serve warm in bowls, with Honey Cream.*

*HONEY CREAM:

Beat 1 cup whipping cream until thick. Add 1/2 teaspoon ground cinnamon and 2 Tablespoons honey. Beat well.

CREAMY PEACH ICE CREAM

gelato di pesche

Cooking Time: 18 minutes
Utensils: 4-quart glass mixing bowl
Servings: Makes 4 quarts

2 cups light cream (half and half)
2 cups whipping cream
4 egg yolks
1/4 teaspoon salt
2/3 cup sugar

1. In a 4-quart bowl microwave light cream and whipping cream on **HIGH (100%) 7 to 8 MINUTES**, stirring once. Beat egg yolks, salt and sugar until light and lemony in a small bowl. Beat a small amount of hot cream into egg mixture and then blend back into cream. Microwave on **HIGH (100%) 10 MINUTES** or until custard just begins to thicken, stirring at 2-minute intervals. Pour into a 4-quart ice cream freezer and refrigerate to cool.

3 pounds fresh peaches, peeled, seeded and chopped (4 cups)
2/3 cup sugar
1 Tablespoon lemon juice
1 teaspoon almond extract

2. Chop peaches finely in food processor or blender. Stir in sugar, lemon juice and almond extract. Stir peaches into cooled ice cream mixture and follow freezer instructions.

PEAR DATE DELIGHT

délice de dattes et de poires

Cooking Time: 10 minutes 30 seconds
Utensils: 1-cup measure
8 x 8-inch glass dish
Servings: 6

3 pears, peeled, halved and cored
1/4 cup chopped dates

1. Arrange pear halves, sliced side up, in an 8 x 8-inch dish. Fill centers with dates.

1 Tablespoon margarine
1 Tablespoon orange juice
1 Tablespoon light corn syrup
Nutmeg for sprinkling

2. In a 1-cup measure melt margarine on **HIGH (100%) 30 SECONDS**. Add orange juice and corn syrup. Pour over pear halves and dates. Sprinkle with nutmeg. Cover with wax paper and microwave on **HIGH (100%) 10 MINUTES**, basting at 2-minute intervals. Serve warm with a dollop of whipped cream.

CREAMY FRUIT FROST

Utensil: Food Processor
Servings: 6

1 cup whipping cream
1/3 cup sugar

1. Blend whipping cream and sugar quickly in the food processor with the steel blade, not too long as mixture will turn to butter.

1 pound frozen fruit (Choose one of the following: strawberries, sliced peaches, blackberries, raspberries, blueberries or sliced bananas.)

2. With machine running, drop frozen fruit into the feeder tube, processing until the 1 pound of frozen fruit has been added. Process until smooth. Spoon into individual serving dishes. Freezes well, too.

"Waves and Blades" co-author, Patsy Swendson, sent this delightful and quick food processor dessert to serve with microwave meals!

STRAWBERRIES SAVANNAH FLAMBÉ

fraises flambées savanna

Over ice cream!

Cooking Time: 3 minutes 30 seconds
Utensils: 1½-quart glass serving dish
Chafing dish stand, optional
2-cup glass measuring cup
Servings: 4–6

2 baskets fresh strawberries (about 3 cups)

1. Rinse and remove stems from strawberries. Place whole berries in flame-proof 1½-quart serving dish. (Dish could be placed in chafing dish stand with burner for table-side flambé.)

6 Tablespoons honey
2 Tablespoons margarine
1/4 cup Amaretto di Saronno liqueur

2. Place honey and margarine in a 2-cup measure. Microwave on **HIGH (100%) 1 MINUTE 30 SECONDS**. Add Amaretto and continue to microwave on **HIGH (100%) 2 MINUTES**.

1/4 cup 151 proof rum for flaming, plus 1 metal tablespoon of rum to ignite

3. Pour hot syrup over strawberries and add rum. Ignite metal tablespoon of rum, then using the tablespoon, ignite strawberry mixture. Serve plain or over vanilla ice cream.

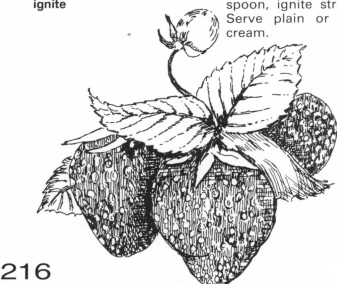

MEXICAN BREAD PUDDING

capirotada a la mexicana

Cooking Time: 13 minutes
Utensils: 1½ or 2-quart round glass dish with a center post
2 (4-cup) glass measuring cups
Servings: 6

2 cups milk
**1 (3-oz.) package cream
cheese, cubed and
softened**
**5 slices toasted white bread,
cubed**

1. In a 4-cup measure stir together milk and cream cheese. Microwave on **HIGH (100%) 4 MINUTES**, stirring once. Place bread cubes in a buttered round dish. Pour hot milk mixture over cubes and let soak 10 minutes.

1/4 cup margarine
1 cup brown sugar
1 teaspoon nutmeg
1½ teaspoons cinnamon
1/4 teaspoon salt
3 eggs, well beaten

2. Micromelt margarine in a 4-cup measure on **HIGH (100%) 1 MINUTE**. Stir in brown sugar, nutmeg, cinnamon, salt and beaten eggs. Mix well.

1 teaspoon vanilla
1/4 cup pecans, chopped
1/2 cup seedless raisins

3. Add vanilla, pecans and raisins. Pour mixture over bread crumbs and stir lightly until blended. Microwave on **HIGH (100%) 7–8 MINUTES**. Rotate dish 3 or 4 times. Let stand 5 to 10 minutes before serving. Servings may be spooned or sliced.

CHOCOLATE MOUSSE

mousse au chocolat

Cooking Time: 2 minutes
Utensils: 4-cup glass measuring cup
          6 pots de crème or demitasse cups
Servings: 6

**6 ounces semi-sweet
   chocolate squares
2 Tablespoons Kahlúa liqueur
1 Tablespoon orange juice**

**2 eggs
2 egg yolks
1/2 cup sugar
1 teaspoon vanilla
1 cup whipping cream**

1. Melt chocolate squares in Kahlúa and orange juice in a 4-cup measure on **MEDIUM (50%) 2 MINUTES**. Stir at 1-minute intervals until chocolate is melted.

2. In a blender place 2 eggs and 2 egg yolks, sugar and vanilla. Blend on high 2 minutes. Add cream and blend on medium 30 seconds. Blend in chocolate mixture. Pour in pots de créme cups or demitasse cups. Refrigerate. Serve with a dollop of whipped cream on top.

OZARK PUDDING

Cooking Time: 7 minutes
Utensils: 9-inch glass pie plate
Servings: 4

1 egg
3/4 cup sugar
1/2 teaspoon vanilla

1. Beat the devil out of one egg. Add sugar and vanilla.

2 heaping Tablespoons all-purpose flour
1 teaspoon baking powder
Dash of salt

2. Mix flour, baking powder and salt in a small dish. Add to egg mixture.

1 large apple, peeled or unpeeled, cored and chopped in small cubes
1/2 cup pecans, broken
Ice cream or whipped cream, optional

3. Add apple and pecans to mixture. Place in a 9-inch buttered pie plate and microwave on **HIGH (100%) 7 MINUTES**. Rotate dish at 2-minute intervals. Spoon into serving dishes and serve with ice cream or whipped cream.

DIVINITY
fondant divin

Cooking Time: 17 to 19 minutes
Utensils: 8-cup glass measuring cup
Servings: 30 pieces

3 cups sugar
1/2 cup light corn syrup
2/3 cup water

1. In an 8-cup measure combine sugar, corn syrup and water. Microwave on **HIGH (100%) 17 to 19 MINUTES** until mixture reaches hard-ball stage 260°.*

1/4 teaspoon salt
2 egg whites
1/4 teaspoon vanilla extract
1 cup pecans, broken

2. Add salt to egg whites in a large mixing bowl and beat on high speed with electric mixer until stiff peaks form. Slowly pour syrup in a thin stream into egg whites, beating constantly until mixture loses its gloss and thickens, about 4 or 5 minutes. Stir in vanilla and nuts. Drop at once by spoonfuls onto foil.

*MICRO MEMO:

*Microwave candy probes and microwave candy thermometers are available for high temperature use during microwave cooking only. A conventional or regular candy thermometer can be used **only** when the microwave is **"OFF"** to check the temperature of the recipe.*

FANTASTIC FUDGE
gianduia fantastica

Cooking Time: 7 minutes
Utensils: 8-cup glass measuring cup
            7 x 11-inch glass baking dish
Servings: 3 dozen squares

1⅔ cups sugar
1/2 cup evaporated milk

1. Combine sugar and milk in an 8-cup measuring cup or bowl. Microwave on **MEDIUM HIGH (70%) 4 MINUTES**. Stir well and continue to microwave on **MEDIUM HIGH (70%) 3 MINUTES** or until boiling and sugar dissolves.

12 ounces milk chocolate
    pieces (semi-sweet
    chocolate, butterscotch
    bits or a combination of
    the two may be
    substituted)
2 cups miniature
    marshmallows
1 teaspoon vanilla
Dash of salt
1 cup chopped pecans

2. Add chocolate, marshmallows, vanilla, salt and pecan pieces stirring until chocolate and marshmallows are melted. Pour into buttered glass dish. Cool and cut into squares.

LECHE QUEMADA

A sweet treat

Cooking Time: 16 minutes
Utensils: 12-inch glass plate
         8-cup glass measuring cup
         8-inch square glass dish
Servings: 36 squares

2 cups pecans, small or broken

1. "Roast" pecans on a large glass plate on **HIGH (100%) 8 MINUTES**, stir and rearrange pecans at 2-minute intervals so pecans will not burn. Set aside.

1/2 cup margarine

2. In an 8-cup measure melt margarine on **HIGH (100%) 1 MINUTE**.

2/3 cup brown sugar, packed
1 cup sweetened condensed milk

3. Stir in brown sugar and condensed milk. Microwave on **HIGH (100%) 7 MINUTES**, stirring at 2-minute intervals so mixture will not burn.

1 teaspoon vanilla (Mexican vanilla if available)

4. Beat until stiff. Add vanilla and roasted pecans. Mix together and spread in a greased 8-inch square dish. Chill, cut into squares then continue to chill until firm. *¡Muy Bueno!*

PEANUT BUTTER SIGHS

dulces de crema de maní

Cooking Time: 3 minutes 30 seconds
Utensils: 7 x 11-inch glass baking dish
          Flat glass dish or paper plate
Servings: 45 squares

1 (8-oz.) jar natural peanut butter, no salt
1 cup margarine
1 pound confectioners powdered sugar

1. Place peanut butter and margarine in a 7 x 11-inch baking dish. Cover with wax paper and microwave on **HIGH (100%) 2 MINUTES**, until margarine and peanut butter melt. Blend together. Add powdered sugar stirring to mix. Press smoothly into bottom of dish.

1 (12-oz.) package semi-sweet chocolate chips

2. Place chocolate chips in a flat dish to melt on **HIGH (100%) 1 MINUTE 30 SECONDS**. Spread over top. Cool in refrigerator and cut into squares.

PRALINES À L' ORLÉANS

Cooking Time: 13 minutes
Utensils: 4-quart glass mixing bowl
Servings: 40 pralines

1 cup whipping cream
1 pound light brown sugar

1. Mix cream and brown sugar together in a 4-quart bowl. Microwave on **HIGH (100%) 13 MINUTES** (stirring not necessary). Candy thermometer reading should be 227° soft-ball stage.

2 cups pecan halves
2 Tablespoons margarine,
  room temperature

2. Quickly add pecans and margarine stirring to mix. Drop candy by teaspoons onto a sheet of foil.

SWEET POTATO PRALINES

pralines de patates

Smooth and delicious

Cooking Time: 25 minutes and 43 seconds
Utensils: 4-quart Pyrex mixing bowl
Servings: 30-40 pralines

3 cups granulated sugar
1/2 cup liquid brown sugar
1 cup evaporated milk
1 (17-oz.) can sweet
potatoes, drained and
mashed
Dash salt

1. In a 4-quart Pyrex mixing bowl combine sugar, brown sugar, milk, mashed sweet potatoes and salt; mix well. Microwave on **HIGH (100%) 25 MINTUES 43 SECONDS** until mixture reaches soft-ball stage 235°. (Drop 1/2 teaspoon of candy mixture into very cold water. When a soft ball forms and flattens on removal from water, the correct stage has been reached.)

2 cups pecans, small halves
or broken large

2. When sweet potato mixture has reached 235°, add pecans; mix well. Drop by spoonfuls onto a sheet of foil. Cool.

Converted to microwave cooking from a recipe contributed by the Louisiana Sweet Potato Commission.

The following friends submitted recipes which were developed and tested for microwave cooking. Ten recipes submitted had been converted to microwave cooking, all others were converted in the Tout de Suite kitchen.

Carol Allen
Senator Nelson Allen
Barbara Arceneaux
Anita Atkins
Mildred Becker
Joan Beckert
Joanne Beckmann
Helen Bernhardt
Mrs. Steve Berniard
Don Biggs
Sharon Biggs
Becky Bishop
Claire Bohn
Judy Boutte
Nancy Bradley
Schautze Brammell
Maldry Breaux
Joe Broussard
Katherine B. Broussard
Linda Burke
Betty Butcher
Carolyn Camardelle
Elaine Carol
Mary Lou Carman
Ann Chenoweth
Nell Clark
JoAnn Coats
Lucille R. Copeland
Dr. Albert Corne
Mary Beth Cyvas
Eva Dell Daigre
John Daigre
Celia Darsey
Dona Davis
Doris Dayton
Marco de Grazia
Mabel de la Rosa
Linda Domingue
Debbie Doughty

Dora Durkee
Joan S. Falgoust
*Doris Farrell
Ginny Foster
Lucile Freeman
Pat Freeman
Johnnie Gachassin
Jean Gage
Penny Gaido
Dorothy Gerdsen
Eloise Gerhardt
Jean Gibson
*Mary Lib Guercio
Tommy Guercio
Ray Halsey
Wanda Ham
Mary Elizabeth Hamilton
Pat Hance
Louise Hanchey
Dorman Haymon
Billie Hebert
Marilyn Hoffpauir
Betty Hollingsworth
*Verlie House
Bebe Inkley
Theresa Jones
*Lucy S. Kellner
Lorraine Keowen
Patsy Kincaid
Susan Lafferty
Dorothy Lampshire
Ann LeJuene
Womack LeJuene
Catherine Levermann
Dutch Levermann
*Jolene Levermann
Betsy Magee
Dottie Manion
Margaret McCoy

Sue McDonough
Mac McJimsey
Shirley McKaskle
M I C H A E L
Louise Mickler
Libby Miller
Sue Ann Mills
Ileta Moore
*Sally Moores
Mona Mouton
Mickey Newton
Lillian Nugent
LaVonne Owen
Janice C. Parra
Jo Ann Patterson
Ginger Pecorino
Shirley Picou
Babs B. Prentice
Sis Rich
Jane Riley
Carolyn Richard
Connie Cromwell
Marianne Schneider
Kirk Schlein
Dot Sevier
Ann Steiner
Ida Hillard Stevens
Patsy Swendson
Alyce Tatum
Tina Thibaut
Judy Trammell
*Cindy Traugott
Louise Webre
Katie Wheeler
Cici Williamson
*Maxine Willis
Margaret Womack
Conway Yarbrough
Melanie Yarbrough

*Group of companions attending the Chateau Country Cooking School with Jean Durkee.

INDEX